Discovering the Soul

Discovering the Soul

The Amazing Findings of a Psychiatrist and His Patients

by Robert G. Jarmon, M.D.

with a Foreword by
Raymond A. Moody, Jr., M.D.

Brighton Productions
Spring Lake, New Jersey

Brighton Productions
P.O. Box 755
Spring Lake N.J. 07762

www.jarmon.com

Library of Congress Cataloging-in-Publication Data
    Jarmon, Robert G.
    Discovering the soul : the amazing findings of a psychia-
trist and his patients / by Robert G. Jarmon
        p.   cm.
    Includes bibliographical references.
    ISBN 0-87604-370-8
    1. Hypnotic age regression—Therapeutic use—Case stud-
ies. I. Title
RC499.H96J37   1996
616.89'162-DC20   96-38945

Cover Background
"Colliding Galaxies" by Carol Benton

Dedication

This book is dedicated to all of those other souls who have made and will make part of my journey with me so that I may learn what I need to learn so that I may do whatever it is that I am supposed to do during this lifetime.

Especially to my father, Albert Jargowsky, for the easy lessons, to my mother, Helen Pisarowicz, for the difficult lessons, and to my wife, Mary, for making the journey a joy.

Special Thanks

I would like to thank my good friends and colleagues who gave of their time and talents, critiquing this work: Suzanne Carmody, R.N., and Robert Elman who reminded me of all those elements of writing that evaded my attention in school.

I also thank my youngest son, Nicholas, who exercised the patience of Job trying to teach his daddy how to store, retrieve, edit, and print this manuscript on our computer.

Contents

Foreword by Raymond A. Moody, Jr., M.D. .... *ix*
Preface .... *xiii*
Introduction .... *xv*

Part I
How We Form and Re-form Our Beliefs

1   Mother's Rainbow 1
2   The Changing of Minds 5
3   Lessons from the Firewalk 22
4   Clinical Hypnosis 29

Part II
Case Studies

5   When Anna Was Elizabeth 37
6   A Reunion of Ancient Colleagues 44
7   The Night Screamer 52
8   Forgotten Injuries 56
9   Comatose but Still Listening 63
10   Claustrophobic Since Birth 69
11   Help from an Old Friend 78
12   Doing Penance 84
13   NDE—Eavesdropper 91
14   NDE—The Reluctant Returner 98
15   Leaving the Body for a Clearer View 102
16   Summoning Help from Loved Ones 109
17   Fatherly Advice—From the Departed 114
18   The Old Fireman 122
19   Useless Tubing 127
20   Healed by an Unknown Persona 133
21   The Lonely Shepherd Persona 140
22   Terror Under a Full Moon 148
23   The Woman Who Hated Money 156

Part III
The Ongoing Search

24   The Lesson of a Loser 165
25   Reflections on Mass-Hypnosis Regression 171
26   Spirit Attachment and Spirit Releasement
        Therapy 176
27   Karmic Interludes and the Road Ahead 187
Epilogue *197*
Notes *211*
Bibliography *213*

✧ Foreword

The opportunity to write the foreword for this book has come to me through a fortuitous triangulation of wonderful people whom I love. The author, Dr. Bob Jarmon, has been a friend for years. I got to know him through Dr. Brian Weiss in conjunction with our speaking engagements at the Association for Research and Enlightenment (A.R.E.), in Virginia Beach, Virginia. Bob is a fine, thoughtful person with great common sense. My wife Cheryl and I often comment that the Weisses are just about the sweetest, funniest people we know. Connecting us all together are the warm, considerate folks at A.R.E., who have supported my work through thick and thin for many years.

As medical doctors, people like to keep us in pigeon-holes, but since I have so much fun exploring new ideas,

I'm often in hot water with the old guard. For twenty years, however, A.R.E. has graciously given me a forum to present my unusual ideas on a wide variety of topics. No matter how new each successive idea has seemed, A.R.E. was ready to listen with an open mind and always came through with, "OK. Sounds great. Let's do it." Words like those are music to an explorer's ears. It is in that same spirit of openness to new ideas that A.R.E. has published this fine book.

In this brief foreword, I am hereby declaring my own independence from the old ways of arguing and disputing about the paranormal. What passes for scholarship about this subject seldom makes any real progress. The fact is that the controversy has been deadlocked since antiquity. The very framework of argumentation has been inadequate, apparently monopolized by three schools of thought.

Modern parapsychologists struggle to fulfill the false promise that someday the scientific method, or some other rational procedure, will "prove" or provide empirical evidence for life after death, ESP, or precognition. The "scientific skeptics," who aren't really skeptics at all, are otherwise well-meaning scientists who think they have all the answers; paranormal experiences, they believe, are easily explainable as wishful thinking, hoaxes, or mixed-up brain chemistry. The third category comprises those fundamentalists of philosophical and religious thought, who, through self-righteous judgment, would condemn anyone who dares to explore the paranormal, searching for demons behind every unexplainable phenomenon.

The fact is that all three groups have shared equally in their inadequacy to discover the truth about the paranormal. Aside from their inherent prejudices, the use of inadequate language has been primary among their impediments. What has been required, and quietly unfolding over the past several years, has been a new breed of investigator, one who has all the benefits of a scientific education, along with spiritual honesty and open-minded inquiry. Here, I cite the work of Dr. Weiss, my own contribution, whatever that may be, and, of course, the work of Dr. Jarmon.

This new trend has opened the door to an entirely new way of studying the paranormal. In my own work toward understanding the paranormal, I have discovered an effective new approach I call "playful paranormalism." But don't be fooled by the name, because it is a serious, scholarly approach to the subject which holds that it is safely and reliably possible to recreate paranormal experiences (apparitions of the deceased and near-death experiences, etc.) so they can be studied systematically. Already, for example, by applying the principles of "playful paranormalism" to the study of the ancient Greek oracles of the dead, I have devised a method that enables subjects to have vivid, first-hand visionary reunions with departed loved ones. Several psychologists in the U.S. and Europe have confirmed the results.

With new techniques such as mine, and the cutting-edge work presented in this book, the day is fast approaching when people will no longer need to get their information about the paranormal second-hand, by hearing it from others. There will one day be a system in place that will enable everyone to observe their own paranormal experiences. Ordinary people will be in a position to make up their own minds about the paranormal, and at that point the three stuffy old systems of thinking about the paranormal will be obsolete. We will no longer have to hear about it from the "experts"; we will have our own personal experiences upon which to reflect.

Dr. Jarmon's book is a good example of the new direction in which the study of the paranormal is moving.

What he writes is a plain demonstration that we ordinary folk can recognize and understand life-changing, paranormal, and spiritual experiences. I like his way of proceeding: show people that the paranormal is accessible, and permit them to open up to the extraordinary alternate realities that are an important part of being human.

Thanks again to Bob Jarmon, Brian Weiss, and the A.R.E. I'm looking forward to our continuing friendship and love for a long time to come.

Raymond Moody, M.D.
October 1996

✧ Preface

As a physician writing a book on psychotherapeutic techniques, I was warned to not use the word *God*, as that would undermine (if not outright destroy) my credibility and risk making me sound like an evangelist in sheepskin clothing. My apologies to those who take offense at the "G" word, but I could find no legitimate nor convenient way around it. I toyed with trying to give God a scientific pseudonym such as "Universal Energy Pool," the "Omni Factor," the "Ubiquitous Cosmic Force Field," etc., but all of those terms seemed blatantly too cumbersome. So *God* it is.

As you read this book and I share with you my observations and thoughts about giving attention to the soul in psychotherapy, some of you will undoubtedly find yourselves skeptical or even taking offense as science attempts to trod on religion's turf. In my practice the questions that often arise with this treatment approach relate to religious heresy, scientific provability, and therapeutic efficacy.

As to the first concern, whether or not a person should be labeled a heretic or infidel is, of course, purely a function of who is doing the labeling.

As to the second concern, we will see that much, if not most, if not all of this theory evades scientific methodology (as is true of most of what we take for granted as valid).

As to the last concern, "Does this really work?" the answer is a resounding . . . "Often."

✧ Introduction

This book concerns something which most of us have been hearing about since early childhood—the soul. It concerns the major importance of addressing the needs (sometimes the anguished cries) of the soul in psychiatric practice.

I am a physician, licensed to practice in the State of New Jersey where I have served on my hospital staff for over eighteen years and where I also have an active psychiatric practice. Although I began my career as a specialist in emergency medicine, I have provided psychiatric counseling for two decades and have specialized in psychiatry since 1987. However, I am not going to discuss the long-accepted principles and theories of psychiatry, psychoanalysis, or the contributions of such pioneers as Freud, Jung, Adler, and others whose beliefs were disdained at one time as metaphysical "nonsense."

I am going to share what I have learned about the nature of the soul, or spirit; about the survival of the spirit after death; and its re-appearance in successive lives—reincarnation, in the parlance of some religions; and about the manifestations of the spirit entities after their bodies have died.

I will also share with you the applications of these concepts in my approach to psychiatric healing, often in conjunction with the now more widely accepted tools of hypnoanalysis and hypnotic regression.

I will recount therapy sessions in which hypnotic regression enabled patients to relive the positive and negative experiences of childhood and even early infancy. Some of these patients, in fact, appeared to regress *beyond their present lives to past lives*. In doing so, they came to understand and conquer mysteries, disorders, or deeply troubled feelings that had prevented them from living their present lives in joyous fullness.

Whether the underlying concepts of the soul and the afterlife can ever be definitively confirmed (or are even valid) may be irrelevant to healing effectiveness. If therapy works, it works—if, that is, it effects a healing and not merely a concealment or substitution of symptoms. Quite simply, it does work.

It must also be admitted that a holistic approach to therapy—taking into account the whole human being, *including the invisible, intangible,* but supremely important soul—is not a cure all. Certainly, not all problems are purely or even mostly spiritual in nature. There are many psychiatric disorders that require very well-established therapeutic interventions, and some disorders are incurable, some sufferings unavoidable.

Yet, it is also true that the mind, spirit, and emotions strongly influence a great many human disorders and illnesses, physical as well as mental, and the goal of healing ought to always be *total* healing.

*   *   *

I did not always follow this startling, sometimes even frightening path. I came to it in gradual steps, first by studying and practicing psychiatry, then by adding hypnosis to my therapeutic arsenal, and finally encountering phenomena difficult if not impossible to explain in any terms but the spiritual.

The nature of the soul has always been and still is a mystery to me. My questions about it have changed through the years. At first I asked, is it real? Is it tangible, and if so, where is it located? Does it have a visible manifestation? What color is it? What will happen to it when I die? Do animals have souls? Are there people without souls?

Gradually, my questions became more sophisticated—or "scientific." Does the soul represent a hitherto unmeasured energy wave form? Does it fit into any paradigm of traditional Newtonian physics? Is it merely a stratagem of the fearful mind, created by us to give hope for existence beyond inevitable death? If it does exist, what influence might it exert on a patient's physical or emotional health?

A major obstacle in acknowledging the existence of the soul, or spirit, in the construct of human pathology is the problem of measuring or quantifying it. Where under the microscope or at the autopsy table can a medical student see it? How can we even be sure it exists?

Most of the time (note that I did not say *all the time*) it is invisible, and invisibility naturally arouses skepticism. Does it exist? Did barometric pressure exist before 1643 when Torricelli invented the barometer? Did ultraviolet and infrared light exist before we could measure them?

By the same logic, should I ignore a patient's accounts

of anything whose reality I cannot prove? Perhaps we should abandon analgesics with their potential adverse side effects. After all, I have never *seen* a patient's pain. If I cannot test and measure it objectively, how can I know it exists?

Another problem in dealing with the concept of the soul is that by merely speaking of it we begin to sound like religious disciples or evangelists. Religion and medicine are supposed to have gone their separate ways centuries ago. No longer do most civilizations have their healers, who at one time ministered to the body and soul together, recognizing no clear delineation. Such healers are the equivalent of modern therapists who dare to look at the entire person, mind-body-spirit, and prescribe accordingly. The holistic approach is much more difficult today, although fortunately there are therapists who practice it. One obstacle to it is sheer volume of medical knowledge, which has become too voluminous for any one practitioner to know in its entirety. We, therefore, tend to concentrate only on physical—observable, testable, or measurable—aspects of a given problem (or set of problems), bringing to bear our specialized (thus limited) training. Other aspects, being harder to detect and harder still to comprehend, are ignored. But a patient is something more than a malfunctioning machine, and we must be something more than mechanics.

I was not always so spiritual in my clinical approach, and I did not at first understand how hypnosis could aid a therapist in a form of exploratory spiritual surgery—cutting beneath the conscious to explore the subconscious and a host of hidden memories going back in some instances to birth and even beyond to past lives.

In our last year of medical school, students were assigned to research some esoteric aspect of medicine as it related to one of our patients. I had a patient afflicted with amyotrophic lateral sclerosis (ALS, Lou Gherig's

Disease). In searching the medical literature for possible treatments, I read about the experiences of the few clinicians who were using hypnosis to improve the quality of life and martial the internal strengths of patients suffering from debilitating or terminal diseases. Hypnosis, I learned, could physiologically alter body functions such as blood flow, pain response, and involuntary muscle movement.

The American Medical Association had recommended in the 1950's that hypnosis be taught in medical schools, but very few physicians were using it.

I have come to know other psychiatrists who are using hypnotic techniques to try to gain understandings of their patients' souls.

Whether or not you accept the concepts in this book is up to you. Here, I will retell these case studies as I would to any of my colleagues in a medical conference. All of these reports are real. I have changed the details only enough to maintain patient anonymity. In aggregate, they lead me to a wonderful realization of my own role as a physician in this life. See what conclusions you come to as you hear my patients' stories.

PART I

HOW WE FORM AND
RE-FORM OUR BELIEFS

1 ✧ Mother's Rainbow

Dealing with people's lives can be humbling and disquieting for all of us in the healing professions. So much faith is placed in us, yet there is so much we do not understand and cannot control. It is dismaying to realize that *every* human being inevitably must say or do things that have a direct effect on some other person's life or, in rarer instances, even on another person's acceptance of death. In the latter situation, our own attitudes concerning death, and the attitudes of fellow survivors, may also be deeply influenced.

Such occurrences are all the more unsettling when we are dealing with our own families. Still, in all these dealings there are lessons to be learned. I believe I learned something of lasting importance from an experience that took place long before I became a psychiatrist, though much time would pass before I could put the lessons to clinical use.

The year 1979 was terrible for my family. My mother-in-law was suffering from breast cancer. She came home from the hospital to die, for the cancer had metastasized throughout her body, even into her bones, and there was no possibility of recovery.

The cancer in her bones made the slightest bodily movement excruciating. I had studied and begun to practice hypnosis, and now I tried to ease her pain with hypnotic analgesia, but my initial attempts were disheartening. She could not at first accept my efforts without resistance. A devout Catholic who had raised her fifteen children in "the faith," she gently, gratefully tolerated my attempts, but said in a voice that did not falter, "God must have a reason for my pain, and He alone can ease it."

Ultimately, I was able to give her some relief by having her transfer the image of her own pain to the image of Christ's suffering on the cross, couched in the format of prayer. Of course, I did not tell her that imagining a transfer of pain is a common technique in medical hypnosis. That would have done her no good, and I was thankful for any help I could provide.

That same week, my father entered the hospital with his fourth heart attack. My mother-in-law, weakening and in recurring pain, said she would pray for him to get well quickly. When I told Dad, he said, "Thank her for me, Bob, and tell her to concentrate on praying for herself—I'll get through this all right." A few days later, I dragged myself home after a twelve-hour tour of night duty at a hospital to learn that my father had just died.

My mother-in-law was a woman of exceptionally strong constitution, but over the next two months her condition continued to deteriorate. Finally, she became too weak even to sip liquids. The time had come for the

doctors and family to make a painful decision—her
agony would not be prolonged by administering intravenous fluids. She slipped into a coma with no further
attempts at therapy.

The family gathered from distant points, and a death
watch began. For two days, her blood pressure hovered
at 40 palpable, with labored breathing. Her strength had
always been beautiful, and it had not been squandered.
She was clinging to her painful existence with every fi-
ber of her tormented being. The children were exhausted. At such a time, as many readers can confirm
from their own grieving experiences, there is no shame
in wishing or praying for the end to come.

Remembering my previous observations of a comatose patient at the hospital, I gathered the family to her
bedside and told them I believed the end was close. "If
there's anything you want to say to Mother, I think you
should tell her now. She's too weak to answer, but I believe she can still hear you." For those left behind, it can
be very important to say a few last words to express their
love and make their peace.

Several members of the family spoke their final words
to her, and when all who wished to speak had done so, I
took her hand. "It's all right, Mother," I said. "It's all right
for you to go now." Her pale, withered lips seemed to
tighten with resolve, and her head turned slightly, as if in
defiance of death.

One of her sons, Gregory, gently took her other hand
and spoke to her again. "It's okay, Mother. We all love you,
and we release you. You've done your work." Her daughter Margaret softly added a few words, confirming what
Gregory had said.

"You can go to your rest now, Mother," I said. "We all
love you, and we'll be with you soon, soon enough."

With that, her breathing stopped. Someone had left
the television set on in the next room, and her favorite

movie, *The Wizard of Oz,* was being aired. At the moment she died, we could hear the melody of her favorite song, "Over the Rainbow."

The next day was cold and drab. Several of us were standing in the living room, talking only intermittently. A moment came when there was complete silence as we faced the large picture window and gazed out over the dark ocean. Then, one by one, we became aware of a gentle light brightening the room. Forming an arc over the sky was an enormous rainbow, and above and behind it, a secondary one. None of us could speak. At last, as the primary rainbow began to shift and fade, one of the children softly voiced the thought that had taken hold of all of us.

"It's Mother—she's made it over—she's telling us it's OK, to be at peace."

Still spellbound, we nodded our heads.

Two days later, my wife Mary was clearing away medications and various other items on Mother's nightstand. Onto the floor fell that week's missalette—a collection of devotions—which the priest had left for her a few days before. On its cover was a rainbow and the words, "The bow in the sky shalt be thy covenant."

Many years have passed, and still my voice falters when I tell people this story. Mother provided me with a lesson about the healing arts which I had missed in my medical training and experience—a lesson beyond that which we can measure in a laboratory or on an autopsy table. Beyond the measurable there exists a mind-body-spirit connection that we can be open to, though not fully understand.

Thanks, Mom.

2 ✧ The Changing of Minds

Rarely does a single experience totally change a person's views of life, death, and the possibilities of all that lies before and after. Rather, there are cumulative effects on one's views, built on a foundation of many experiences. Some of these experiences may be as dramatic as the rainbow that marked my mother-in-law's passage to the afterlife. Others may be subtle—may even seem unimportant if not trivial at the time it happens; yet, we are all the sum of our pasts.

In the introduction to this book, I remarked that I was not always so spiritual in my clinical approach, and I enumerated some impediments to the acceptance of the spiritual factor as a component of any problem to be treated. I wrote of skepticism, the limitations of classroom and clinical training, and the almost unmanageable scope of information (all of it dealing with physical or mental phenomena, excluding the soul) that must be mastered by a medical practitioner even within a narrow field of specialization. Still another very practical obstacle is the medical procedure code, which alone might have blocked my progress toward the spiritual if I had been more impressed by the system than by my experiences with troubled patients.

Used by insurance carriers, the code of procedural designations—which number in the thousands—attempts to ascribe a pigeonhole for every therapeutic intervention. This seems like a logical way (or perhaps the only practical way) to codify and reimburse costs for care rendered. But how do I codify the real, underlying problems of a patient like the widow I shall call Sarah Hawkins, whose nicotine addiction was killing her? I did not "cure" her of the chain-smoking habit (though I succeeded in ending it), because that was merely her chief *symptom*, not her invisible but greater problem.

At sixty-four, Sarah was struggling through her first year of widowhood after forty-two years of marriage. Her husband, also a smoker, had died very suddenly of a heart attack. His departure from life had been sudden and relatively easy; hers might not be.

She had three children and five grandchildren, but only one member of her family lived anywhere near her. Most of her friends had died or moved away or become too ill to enjoy life. She was alone and could no longer discern any purpose in her existence. Cigarettes had become her crutch and her companion—as much a release from reality as hard drugs are for many people, and far more addictive.

Sarah had developed a chronic cough, and still she chain-smoked. My job was to try to save her from lung or throat cancer, emphysema, premature heart attack, or stroke. But most lifelong smokers succeed in conquering the habit only when their desire becomes strong enough—the desire to stop smoking equated with the desire to live. I had to help my patient want to live more than she wanted to die.

Perhaps the yearning to watch her grandchildren grow up, to visit them, and to share with them some of what she had learned in life—perhaps that would give her a strong enough purpose for living. But I sensed that something else was on her mind, something troubling her and thus encouraging her to see a means of "legitimate" suicide.

During the first counseling session, Sarah admitted to me rather hesitantly that two months after her husband's death he had appeared to her. He had stood one night at the foot of her bed—"as real to me, Doctor, as you are. If I had told my kids, they'd think I was crazy. They'd probably put me in a nursing home. I'd rather die."

I asked whether she had told anyone of her vision. Yes, she had told her priest. He had reminded her that when we are in a state of grief, our minds often play strange tricks. He advised her to see a physician if she was troubled again by "apparitions" and added that he would pray for her. Following the priest's advice, she went to her doctor. But when she began to tell the doctor about the visit of her husband's spirit, he cut her short and said he would prescribe something to help her sleep.

"Did your husband talk to you?" I asked. "Did he say anything when he appeared?"

"Just that he's at peace and loves me, and I should be at peace too. But I'm not, Dr. Jarmon. How can I be at peace? Do you know what I want? I want to be with him."

Unlike her priest and her family doctor, I did not shrug off her experience with the easy explanation that the mind plays strange tricks. Indeed it does, as we all know quite well, but who are we to say she was merely imagining that experience? Whether the visitation occurred only in her imagination was hardly relevant to the heal-ing process. What was relevant was to help her realize that her husband's after-death appearance—his assur-ing her that he was at peace—would help her through her time of grief.

I told her about other experiences like hers, in which the spirits of departed loved ones had appeared in order to communicate with someone left behind. Whatever her children might think, there was no reason for her to fear that she was losing her grip on sanity merely be-cause her husband's spirit had come to her and spoken words of comfort. I told her of similar occurrences from other patients of mine, just as I will relate them in this book.

Of course, I also addressed the addiction that had brought her to my office. I counseled her about smok-ing, both then and later when I used hypnosis in her therapy. While she was in trance, I provided spiritually healing affirmations about caring for this temporary body of hers which God had put in her trust and safe-keeping for her soul's journey through this lifetime. I also reinforced her knowledge that her husband's love would continue to warm her during the remainder of her time on earth. The fact that she was still alive indicated that God wanted her here and that there was more work for her to do.

After several therapeutic sessions, she succeeded in breaking her smoking habit, and each day she put away the money she would have spent on three packs of ciga-rettes—saving it so that she could make more trips to see her grandchildren.

This was not one of my most dramatic cases (except in the sense that every success is dramatic), but it illus-trates the point I made about procedural codes being an obstacle to holistic therapy. The claims adjuster at her health-insurance carrier wanted to know if the treatment was for a physical ailment or an emotional disorder. I must admit that I did *not* succeed in explaining that what walked into my office was not merely a pair of traumatized lungs.

At the time Sarah came to me for counseling, I was already predisposed to accept the reality of the spirit—the soul—in one manifestation or another, as it has, does, and will exist before, during, and after the current life of the body. I have conceded that I do not know precisely what constitutes this soul, but I have seen ample evidence that in certain circumstances it expresses itself—takes action of some sort. This indicates that it possesses energy or is, in itself, a form of energy. Indeed, this phenomenon and others related to the psyche are often grouped within a collective term, psychic energy.

Since my beliefs already encompassed the reality of psychic energy, Sarah's experience did not open my eyes to an unfamiliar phenomenon but merely served as another confirmation of that phenomenon. In that sense, I learned nothing that was new to me, but her need for compassionate holistic therapy strengthened my resolve to let no obstacles—not even the procedural categories around which physicians are often forced to maneuver—block my investigations or hamper my clinical approach.

The very laws of physics and thermodynamics that support a mechanistic view (to the exclusion of such mystical concepts as the spirit) hold that energy cannot be destroyed, obliterated, but only altered. Very well. We also know that the brain produces and works with energy—electrical impulses and waves. If psychic energy exists and cannot become nonexistent, what happens to this energy when its temporary housing—the body—ceases to maintain its metabolic functions? That is, what happens to it when we die?

Of course, there are many who do not believe that psychic energy exists in the first place. Since they have not experienced it in some manifestation, and no reputable scientist has yet devised a "psychrometer" to demonstrate its reality, why embrace such a major and unconventional concept? I, for one, would not have until it presented itself to me in various ways. Now that it has, I cannot deny what I have experienced.

Moreover, my experiences have indicated that psychic energy does not invariably or necessarily await bodily death to be released, to take action, to express itself outside of the confines of the body. It may take a variety of forms.

Before entering medical school, I had never considered myself (or perhaps anyone else) to possess any psychic abilities. I had, of course, read about extrasensory perception (ESP), telepathy, clairvoyance, and so on, but considered them nothing more than intriguing theories. More and more often in recent years, investigative and law-enforcement agencies have successfully employed people with exceptional psychic abilities to locate missing persons—or corpses—find hidden evidence, and, thus, to help solve perplexing cases. But none of that had intruded on my personal experience. Then, shortly after I entered medical school, two occurrences challenged and broadened my system of beliefs in how the universe functions.

If a system of beliefs cannot accommodate challenge and potential change, it must be a weak and fearful system. The French essayist Joseph Joubert wisely observed that "those who never retract their opinions love themselves more than they love truth." In our own time—an age of skepticism worshipped as a system of belief—Gloria Steinem has observed that "the first problem for all of us, men and women, is not to learn but to unlearn." My own convictions began to be unlearned during my medical student days.

A good friend, George Bundy, and I had been traveling together frequently, taking a series of airline flights, and now we were to fly from Miami to New York with a brief stop at Fort Lauderdale. As we walked along the airport concourse toward our boarding gate, I was suddenly overwhelmed by a sensation of foreboding. I knew—I knew with certainty—that the plane would not reach its final destination. I hadn't even seen the plane yet, but I knew. Never before had I been nervous about flying, and the feeling of panic was all the stronger for being unfamiliar.

I grabbed my companion's arm and told him we must not board the plane—we had to wait for the next flight. My friend, George, was not only a well-seasoned traveler but a traveler employed in the airplane industry, and he had seen people suddenly, inexplicably, succumb to a fear of flying. Naturally, he tried to reassure me. But when I saw the aircraft, my feeling of impending doom intensified.

"There's something wrong with that plane," I told George, "some structural problem, and there's going to be trouble. I don't know how I know, but it's not going to get us to New York."

During the few minutes before boarding, he questioned me about what I "saw" or sensed. His questions served to focus my mental images more clearly, and I told him I saw no physical harm coming to us or any of the passengers and crew—but I knew the plane had some defect that would abort its flight.

"Come on," George said. "Even if your premonition comes true, you don't see anyone getting hurt. Our bags are on board, so let's go. I never knew you were afraid of flying, but this premonition of yours will make it interesting. And, since you say that we're not going to get hurt, don't you want to see what happens? Let's go."

Go we did. When we took our seats, I still somehow

knew that we would not be injured, yet, I had never in my life been so frightened. It was all the more bewildering because George was right—normally I had no fear of flying. As I boarded the plane, terror set in and would not leave.

At Fort Lauderdale, we sat on the tarmac for thirty minutes, and then George glanced out the window and saw the baggage being unloaded. Soon we were ushered off the plane and told that we would be driven back to Miami, where we would resume our flight on another aircraft.

Just after disembarking, we looked back and saw fuel pouring out of an apparently ruptured tank. It was streaming back close to the jet engines.

There had been no outward sign that anything was wrong with that plane—and, moreover, my premonition had taken hold before I ever saw the plane. At the time, I was undergoing no significant stress, and there was no "logical" explanation for my foreknowledge. Somehow, a message about a future event had come to me from an inanimate object! George could dismiss the occurrence as a coincidence—if admittedly an unlikely coincidence—but I could not and cannot. The only conclusion I could draw was that this universe is somehow much more complicated than my college physics professor would have led me to believe.

About a year later, another such experience challenged and shook my "logical" world. While visiting friends for the weekend, I suddenly knew that someone had died at home. At the same time, I also knew that it was not a member of my family who had died, and I was, therefore, equally bewildered as troubled.

I tried to concentrate, seeking to sense whether someone had died while visiting my family, but I immediately knew that was not the case. Our home included an apartment which we rented out to a tenant. Slowly, I began to sense that it must be the tenant who had died, but the only *strong* sensation I felt was of an unknown person's death.

When I arrived home, my mother told me that the tenant had, indeed, died suddenly and unexpectedly. But how could I have known that someone—anyone—had died? How had that information reached me? What was the nature of the transmission unit, on what sort of wave form did the information travel, what energy source drove it, and what was it in me that received and recognized it? Such experiences are not uncommon, yet people dismiss them, chiefly because they are so disturbing and challenging to what we think we know.

I began to pay more attention to articles and books concerned with extrasensory perception. An article in *Newsweek* mentioned research being conducted on mental telepathy by Douglas Dean, who had been awarded a Nobel Prize for his efforts in helping refugees escape from eastern Europe and who was now a faculty member at Newark College of Engineering—five blocks from my medical school. I phoned Dr. Dean, and he invited me to come over with a friend and participate in an experiment.

My classmate Buz Berlin and I took turns sitting in a room and silently reading, at timed intervals, material that was alternately boring and emotionally charged. While one of us read, the other sat in an adjoining room and had his blood pressure continuously monitored and recorded. Afterward, the type of reading material was compared to changes in blood pressure, and the correlated results indicated that a transmission of emotion was occurring between the two of us—although the person having his blood pressure monitored had no conscious knowledge of what the other person was reading.

To me, this was another piece of evidence supporting the existence of psychic energy—a form of energy that is not addressed in physics texts but is nonetheless real, present, and forceful in its effects on our lives.

I had begun to question my conventional set of beliefs, to unlearn the old and learn the new, to change my mind. Since then, I have observed manifestations of psychic energy in other forms. Those forms have included what we call discarnate spirits, spiritual entities that survive the death of the body and either rest in peace in what we call "the hereafter" or, in certain instances, remain or return to reside in a different body. Indeed, I have heard patients under hypnosis speak of things unknown to them in their present lives, information acquired, perhaps, in past lives, retained by the soul, and unconsciously or subconsciously retrieved from the soul now inhabiting a living body.

All of us are inclined to believe in those things that we are taught from infancy, which our responsible mentors, colleagues, and friends believe, which we see or experience for ourselves, and which fit neatly into our already established concepts (like pieces of a jigsaw puzzle that snap into place to complete a picture).

When Copernicus began his study of astronomy, everyone "knew" the sun revolved around the earth. The science of the times and Mother Church both taught this "fact," which was indeed self-evident. Anyone could gaze at the morning and evening skies and see the sun making its great arc around the earth. Scientists and philosophers had built an entire body of knowledge around that Law of Nature, which dated back to at least 340 B.C. when Aristotle described it in his treatise, *On the Heavens*. In the second century A.D., Ptolemy confirmed and elaborated the same easily accepted concept, which the Church viewed as one of many proofs that the earth was the center of the universe and Man its master, subordinate only to God who had created Man in His image.

But then Copernicus, a Roman Catholic priest, studied the night sky and found that the movements of some heavenly bodies could not be explained on the basis of the accepted earth/sun relationship. Ironically, as far back as the third century B.C., several Greek philosophers had suggested that the earth and other planets revolved around the sun, but their ideas had never been widely accepted. Copernicus reconsidered those ideas, adding to them his own observations and calculations, and from about 1510 to 1514 prepared a manuscript summarizing his new theory. He must have anticipated resistance to such a theory—even outrage among his ecclesiastical superiors—because he circulated the work only among friends, almost secretively. During the next two decades, he continued his studies and gradually began to write and speak more openly about his theory. As expected, there was resistance—probably all the greater because Copernicus came to realize (and declare) that even the sun was not the center of the universe but at some distance from the center of a universe far more immense than anyone had imagined.

The Church during the Renaissance was not, however, as resistant to new ideas as one might suppose. In 1533, Pope Clement VII granted permission for the publication of the principles Copernicus had expounded in lectures given in Rome. But even with the Pope's approval, Copernicus was hesitant, foreseeing quite accurately a reaction of dissent among both clergy and laity. His great and final work, *On the Revolutions of the Celestial Spheres*, was published in the year of his death, 1543, and it initiated the profoundly shocking reformation of scientific theory known as the Copernican Revolution.

While many philosophers and theologians scorned Copernican theory as fantasy—or worse, heresy—a few inquisitive minds investigated and came to accept the new ideas, just as a few (a constantly growing number) today are willing to explore phenomena scorned by skeptics. One such man was Galileo Galilei, a mathematics teacher at the University of Padua, who had come to accept Copernican theory early in life. Galileo, too, was afraid of ridicule (as he stated in a letter to a pioneering astronomer, Johannes Kepler, in 1597) and refrained from public expression of his opinions. Although Galileo did not invent the telescope, he was one of the first to use one to study the skies—and in the skies he saw proofs of the new doctrine, disproofs of the old.

By the time he gathered the courage to lecture and write about his findings, the Inquisition was at the height of its reactionary power, the Church waging a war of ideas and allegiance with the Protestant reform movement, and in 1616 the Vatican issued a decree that Copernicanism was "false and erroneous." All the same, Galileo obtained Papal permission to write about the "systems of worlds"—Ptolemaic versus Copernican— and he did so. His opponents in the Church declared that his writings would have worse consequences "than Luther and Calvin put together."

In 1633 Galileo was tried by the Inquisition, sentenced to house arrest, and forced to spend the remaining eight years of his life in seclusion. (In 1980 the Vatican reopened its assessment of Galileo's work and, after twelve years of studying the matter, determined in 1992 that Galileo was right—that indeed the earth rotated around the sun, and they forgave him.)[1] We condemn the Inquisition not for its cruelty alone but for its obstinate blindness, and yet today we tend to be equally blind to that which does not fit the construct of our conventional set of beliefs.

What about firewalking? Is it possible that ordinary people can step barefoot on coals heated to 1200 degrees Fahrenheit without burning their feet? Can most people believe that? Do *you*? It most definitely does not fit into the Newtonian/Cartesian view of the universe. Nevertheless, firewalking is a reality (see Chapter Three for a description of my own encounter with this "impossibility.")

There are some concepts or ideas that we can comfortably accept without understanding them. Like most people, I believe in Einstein's declaration that $E=mc^2$, not because I understand it—which I do not—but because a great many trustworthy authorities believe it, because its validity has been proved and put to use by scientists, and because it does not threaten my basic belief system. Yet, if tomorrow a *New York Times* article announced that world-renowned nuclear physicists discovered that actually $E=mc^3$, I don't think that would trouble us much. We would accept that as readily as $E=mc^2$ because it had no relevance to our day-to-day existence. When I examine the collection of colorful wires and metal and plastic bits inside my portable radio, I do not understand that either; I do not fully understand how I can hear the evening news broadcast, but I know that the "magic" of the device is not magic, and do not feel that I have to understand how it works before I turn it on and use it.

Most people who have encountered psychic energy believe in its existence, while most of those who have never encountered it do not believe in it. But there is some crossover of belief and non-belief. Sometimes we refuse to believe our own eyes and ears because the information thus received does not fit our accepted set of natural laws. Likewise, at times we are quite willing to accept the reality of a given phenomenon if only because we can observe its effects (though not the phenomenon itself) and/or because we accept the beliefs of a great many other respected rational individuals.

Most people in America today shrug off or scoff at the concept of reincarnation, yet most of the rest of world believes in it. It is a tenet of the major Asian religions, especially Hinduism, Jainism, Sikhism, and Buddhism. It is also a tenet of many sects such as the Druse, an offshoot of Islam. Reincarnation or, at the very least, the survival of the soul is stated or implied in biblical passages and is in accord with ancient Judaic tradition.

Kabbala, a partly oral and partly written system of Jewish mysticism, addresses the concept. Kabbala is a complex interpretation, or collection of interpretations, of the scriptures. The period of greatest activity in compiling and refining it lasted from the twelfth to the sixteenth century, but in its earliest form, the *Merkava*, it flourished in Palestine in the first century A.D. The chief literary product of the *Merkava*, the *Sefer ha-bahir*, compiled in the twelfth century, specifically states the reality of the return of souls: reincarnation.

But what of early Christianity? In the Gospel according to St. John (Chapter One), priests of Jerusalem asked John the Baptist if he was the Prophet Elijah reincarnated, and he said he was not. But Mark presents him as Elijah returned, and Matthew (Chapter Three) emphatically identifies him as Elijah—"he that was spoken of by the prophet Isaiah"—the herald of the Kingdom of God. There is no question that early Christians believed in spirits (such as the spirits of Moses and Elijah, mentioned in the New Testament), angels (mentioned in both Old and New Testaments), the survival of the soul (mentioned often), and its reincarnation. (In II Maccabees, Chapter Seven, there is an account of the martyrdom of a mother and her sons. As they are about to have their hands and feet cut off and their tongues cut out, one of the brothers steps forward, sticks out his tongue and hands and says, "it is from heaven that I received these; for the sake of His laws I disdain them; from Him I hope to receive them again.") Then, at the Council of Nicea in 325 A.D., the powers that were standardizing—or attempting to standardize—Christianity denied reincarnation and expunged references to it. Perhaps they saw in it potential needs of a new cult that might threaten an organized, structured religion and that religion's hierarchy of authority. The concept of transmigration of the soul did not die easily, for a multitude of minds had been changed—opened to it—over many centuries. In the eleventh century, a large sect known as the Cathari or Cathars—an offshoot of Catholicism—arose in western Europe largely in opposition to what they perceived as materialism and corruption in the Church. As their movement spread, it splintered into a number of sub-sects, all of which reinterpreted the scriptures in ways considered heretical. They agreed concerning some beliefs, disagreed about others, but Catharism in its various forms concurred in the reality of reincarnation. As a group, they were often called Albigensians or Albigenses (after Albi, one of their chief centers in the south of France). In 1208, Pope Innocent III enlisted the aid of French noblemen to eradicate the Albigensians, rewarding the aggressors by putting his blessing on lands they confiscated. A crusade was proclaimed, and an army ravaged Toulouse, massacring its inhabitants—both Cathar and Catholic.[2]

More and more scientific researchers are investigating spirit energy and related phenomena. In addition to Dr. Brian Weiss, author of *Many Lives, Many Masters,* Dr. Ian Stevenson of the University of Virginia and Dr. Joseph B. Rhine (whose work at Duke University and at the Institute for Parapsychology has again and again claimed international attention), there are Dr. Gertrude Schmeidler at the College of the City of New York; Dr. William J. Baldwin of the Center for Healing Relationships in Enterprise, Florida; Dr. Raymond Moody, who wrote the Foreword to this book; Larry Dossey, M.D., author of *Recovering the Soul;* and others.

Psychotherapy, however, does not easily lend itself to quantitative measurements and conclusions. Essentially, all theories are just working hypotheses. On the basis of training, experience, and observation, the practitioner makes an apparently logical assumption about the mechanics of behavior. If the problem is solved by putting that assumption or approach into action, it acquires healing value.

The prospect of adding spirituality to the psychic components that must be addressed in psychotherapy sounds like the prospect of adding uncertainty to confusion. Moreover, making assumptions about how the soul or spirit operates—to say nothing of such concepts as spirit entities and angels—sounds dangerously close to trying to explain how God thinks and operates. The notion seems as futile and arrogant as the idea of an ant looking up from the floor of the Sistine Chapel and criticizing Michelangelo's choice of colors. We human beings cannot even ask all the right questions, much less understand the answers if they should be given to us.

Still, it is our nature—our very reason for being, I believe—to ask those questions we *can* ask and to seek enlightenment. Further, I believe that by making full use of spiritual concepts in psychotherapy, some conundrums may be bypassed, and inner peacefulness often achieved by the patient.

Spirit, the often-overlooked component, can underlie many behavioral mysteries and anomalies. Think, for example, about the frequently sharp diversity in personality between siblings. In focusing on whether genetics or environment is more important in determining personality or pathology, we may be overlooking a third piece of the puzzle: the soul with which a person is born, the soul which has been developing through previous existences and experiences.

Just as every physical ailment has (or in some cases

induces) an emotional component, every emotional problem has a spiritual component.

I see a growing trend bringing spirituality back into healing. It may well be that therapy is beginning to fill a need that, all too often, organized religion is no longer meeting adequately.

Perhaps it is enough for now that we have found—stumbled upon, if you prefer—the correct approach and drawn some conclusions that are hard to refute on the basis of the evidence.

Even the F.D.A. does not require that the "mechanism of action" be fully understood before bringing a new product to market—it is enough that the therapy be "safe and efficacious."

Hippocrates said, "Nothing should be omitted in an art which interests the whole world, one which may be beneficial to suffering humanity and which does not risk human life or comfort."

3 ✧ Lessons from the Firewalk

In recounting some of my clinical and personal experiences, I hope I have made it clear that my work has been a constant reminder of the unsolved yet, nonetheless, *useful* mysteries surrounding our lives. In a way, the psyche may be viewed as a microcosm of the cosmos, which teams with phenomena that can be seen, experienced, even tested, but not fully explained by currently known (or currently understood) physical science. Many of these phenomena can be utilized in healing, and even some that are not directly applicable to therapy (as far as I know at this stage of my journey) are useful in demonstrating both the power of the psyche and the infinite range of still unexplained phenomena with answers still to be sought.

When working with therapeutic concepts not fully

embraced by the medical community, caution is essential. *Primum non nocer*—do not harm—is the first rule of medicine. All the same, there must be enough latitude in the system for new, potentially useful modalities to be introduced. Caution implies doubt—which is *not* precisely the same attitude as skepticism. Doubt, in turn, implies faith, and faith implies doubt; and there are times when faith can and should override doubt.

A surgeon may have complete faith in his ability to diagnose appendicitis and remedy it by excision; but until he opens the abdominal cavity and sees the appendix, he cannot truly *know* it is inflamed—he can only surmise. Only when the appendix is removed, biopsied, and when the patient has recovered does he truly know his diagnosis and therapy were correct. Until then, some doubt, however small, has existed, and faith has, therefore, been required.

The skeptic says there are no physical phenomena that cannot be explained by science. The faithful or even the agnostic may counter with a question such as this: What about the so-called crop rings (circles) that have been appearing with increasing frequency in England and Europe and have now been seen on other continents, including North America? Crop rings are conspicuous patterns of flattened or almost flattened grain stems or grasses, usually circular, sometimes forming concentric circles, often forming elaborate designs, that appear almost instantaneously and have been repeatedly investigated and filmed for more than forty years. Our best scientists have insisted that neither wind nor human can possibly produce what he has seen.

Extremely tentative hypotheses have included abrupt changes in the local portion of the earth's magnetic field, some sort of unspecified (and so far unexplained, unknown) solar influence, or a form of communication, or art, or even mere doodling by extraterrestrial visitors! In other words, the phenomenon itself is testable, visible, proved; but it is, as yet, inexplicable by science, a proof that indeed there *are* phenomena which cannot be explained by our current knowledge of science.

Encounters with such phenomena may be daunting to skeptics but are heartening to open-minded investigators who welcome new mysteries that bolster our faith and support our contention that our hypotheses regarding other phenomena are both plausible and reasonable.

I will not dwell on crop rings, since they (apparently) have nothing to do with the psyche, but will recount my own experience with another mysterious phenomenon that most probably bears directly on the psyche. Such experiences lend support to our faith in the validity of the psyche's power and even perhaps in other powers outside of the individual's psyche.

On a hot, humid August evening in 1990, I found myself sitting on a hard metal folding chair in an unfamiliar back room of a church parish center. The scene was common enough at parish centers—a big pot of weak coffee, stacks of doughnuts, and eighteen strangers, aged ten to sixty. But what brought us there was anything but usual. We intended to walk barefoot over a bed of hot coals. As I blotted my brow with a handkerchief and looked about at those people, I asked myself why in the world I had come. Was it merely curiosity? Was it merely an impulse to accept a dare, a challenge?

I confess that both facts must have played a part, but something much more important was involved. I have stressed my firm belief that every person is an inseparable amalgam of body, mind, and spirit, and I work to incorporate this concept into my psychiatric practice as well as my personal life. I say I *work* at it because doubts inevitably creep into one's belief system. While I continually "cheerlead" my patients through emotional/physical ailments, I need to remind myself of the reality of a power and wisdom greater than our own.

A colleague had told me about this meeting; and yes, she had dared me to investigate and try the firewalk for myself. "Bob," she had said, "I think you need to see this firsthand, although I'm not so sure you'll want to participate. The point is, you're always entreating your patients to trust their well-being to a higher power. Now it's your turn—a chance to find out how you really feel about it."

Actually, I needed little persuasion. The practice of firewalking had fascinated me ever since I first read about it. Firewalk rituals or ceremonies have sprung up in isolated cultures around the world, usually as an affirmation of religious faith or spiritual power and protection. Such rituals have been practiced by Cherokees, Tahitians, Tibetans, Hawaiians, Vikings, and Greeks. Now the firewalk was coming to Monmouth County, New Jersey. I wanted to do it not to prove my courage, the way a schoolboy accepts a dare, but because I felt the experience might provide valuable insights and because it seemed to me that if I were to put more faith in the higher power, the higher power would put more faith in me—that is, enable me to function more effectively. Something inside me was insisting: this I will do.

So there we were, nineteen people from various walks of life, listening to a woman in her mid-thirties instruct us how to walk unharmed through the flames. For almost three hours we sat and spoke about overcoming fears, facing life's challenges, breaking self-erected mental and physical barriers. Twice during this time we went outside to build and stoke a bonfire, using a quarter-cord of oak wood, and rake out a sixteen-foot walkway with the glowing embers. At last the young instructor announced, "It's time. Everyone remove your shoes and socks. Now, this is the chant you'll sing to the beating of the drum as we all hold hands around the fire and take turns walking through it. Okay?"

"Okay?" I thought. "I'll chant whatever she wants me to, hold hands with anyone, do whatever she wants, if it will get me across those hot coals!"

We did it. In fact, I did it—three times. A reporter who was there to cover the story laid down his note pad and joined us, and he, too, walked over the red-hot coals. A mother and her quiet ten-year-old son skipped joyfully over the 1,200-degree embers, a miraculous sight. Would this strange experience be of value to that child? Yes, I thought, for the rest of his life he will be undaunted by life's self-imposed limitations, perhaps even immune to such limitations. After all, if one can walk unscathed through fire, can one not ignore or defy other fears and obstacles?

One person did burn his feet, and even his painful experience somehow contained a lesson or insight. A forty-year-old chiropractor who had voiced misgivings throughout the evening, he evidently defeated himself. Or did he? I drove his car home for him because his feet were too burned to use the foot pedals, and I dressed his second-degree burns. But he had seen the phenomenon, had witnessed others as they walked the coals without injury, and had come away knowing more not only about himself but about the potential physical effects of faith. With surprisingly firm resolve, he said he would try it again at the next opportunity.

His injuries and pain were a gift to the rest of us—the gift of reality. It is tempting after the firewalk to disbelieve what you have just experienced, to chalk it up to some relatively easy explanation such as moisture protection from your feet or poor conductivity of the coals, or mass hypnosis, perhaps. Certainly it has nothing to do with moisture or heat conductivity. It would be absurd to believe that either factor would protect eighteen people and fail for the nineteenth. Nothing I have learned in physics or physiology—or, indeed, psychology—can fully explain what we accomplished.

My own reaction was this: when I stepped onto the burning coals, I believed that somehow I was in harmony with the energies of the universe and I would be safe because of that relationship, as untold numbers of other firewalkers had been before me. My burn patient had tried but failed to believe that he would be protected, and, therefore, he was not protected.

Among a sect of Thai Buddhists, there are many people who regard themselves as "spiritual mediums," empowered to bless other believers with the protection of a higher power, and during an annual religious celebration, they affirm their faith by walking on fire and by piercing their flesh with knives, needles, or spikes. The fire does not burn them. Their pierced cheeks, chests, or arms bleed very little, and investigating physicians have been baffled by the speed with which the punctures close and heal. After a day or two, the wound scars are barely visible. Some scientifically qualified observers have hypothesized that this phenomenon is made possible by mass hypnosis or self-hypnosis.

The hypothesis is not unreasonable. Chanting or dancing often precedes a firewalk and may serve as a hypnotic aid; indeed, the Thai firewalkers appear to be in trance. It may also be significant that group action and cohesiveness evidently help people who have not walked the coals before, although many may eventually do it alone. Unquestionably, hypnosis encompasses effects and abilities untapped by most of us and not yet fully understood by any of us. I cannot say that the awe-inspiring and baffling protection afforded by the faith of these people is *not* a form of hypnosis or that the faith itself is not a form of hypnosis. Perhaps. But in that event, my interpretation of the hypnosis itself is that it is a manifestation of being in harmony with the energies of the universe and our own, individual energies. As physicists have said of the atoms that compose us and every particle of matter, essentially we *are* energy—in the form of matter.

I know now that there are laws of this universe operating constantly though we do not fully comprehend them. Perhaps we are not meant to, but that does not mean we should not attempt to put them to work. Meanwhile, there are two courses that we can simultaneously take: one is to continue seeking answers; the other is to put to work principles not fully understood but empirically known to be safe and effective.

Sometimes a patient will say, "I can't," when, for example, discussing quitting smoking or letting go of an old anger. At those times, I find it helpful to point to a photograph on my wall, a souvenir of that night. It shows me walking through the fire. "If the impossible is possible," I say, "then certainly the difficult is do-able."

4 ✧ Clinical Hypnosis

Hypnosis is one of our most ancient healing modalities, and one with an immensely long record of effectiveness; yet, like several other medical approaches, it has come into favor during some periods of history and has fallen from favor during other periods. In this regard, one might cite herbal remedies, acupuncture, placebos, chemical treatment of emotional symptoms, and holistic therapy as examples of modalities that have been similarly acclaimed or disdained at various times and/or in various societies. Ancient though it is, hypnosis still is not universally accepted as an orthodox clinical method, but it is, at last, rapidly gaining that status.

In the ancient cradles of civilization, Persian magi and Greek oracles made use of hypnotic rituals and trances termed *temple sleep*. Hypnotic methods were employed by Assyria-Babylonian physician-priests to exorcise and destroy demons held to be responsible for illness. As early as 500 B.C. (and probably earlier), the Egyptians utilized comparable techniques not only to appease their gods but to promote healing. In general, the ancient methods and hypnotic induction included deep, rhythmic breathing, repetitive prayers and chants, gazing, incense (to stimulate and focus the olfactory sense and establish a calm, receptive state), self-contemplation or yoga-like meditation, and an array of rituals to engender the subject's concentration, cooperation, and expectation—three key elements in establishing a state of hypnosis.

"Modern" hypnosis is generally considered to have been pioneered in 1889 by James Braid, an English physician. It was Braid who coined the term *hypnosis* from the Greek word *hypnos*, meaning sleep. This derivation, unfortunately, leads in large part to the misconception that hypnosis is some type of sleep state, although a person in hypnosis—even deep hypnosis—is not asleep but merely in a state that in superficial aspects resembles sleep.

In 1958 the American Medical Association recommended that all medical schools should include hypnosis training in their curricula.[1] Here is a modality that not only has a wide range of psychotherapeutic uses (from recalling repressed memories to helping a patient program new behavior patterns) but can also affect physical responses. To understand some of the physical implications, consider this: if a person can gag, faint, or wince in pain as a result of what his or her mind perceives, then any illness involving blood flow or nerve-impulse conduction *can be treated at least in part by hypnosis.*

Whether a person is sick or is enjoying good health sometimes depends on a precarious balance between disease-fighting factors (immune response, medications, etc.) and disease-causing factors (bacteria, viruses, faulty circulation, etc.). Visualize a balance scale with precisely ten pounds on one side delicately balancing ten pounds on the other side; the addition or subtraction of just an ounce—or perhaps just a gram—on one side would tip the scale. In therapy, the addition of hypnosis often can provide that ounce or gram of difference.

Caution regarding the unfamiliar is an obvious necessity in the practice of medicine, but it is unfortunate that even now, relatively few physicians have had training in hypnosis. I regard myself as one of the lucky few, because there is no doubt that clinical hypnosis has benefited many of my patients.

Hypnosis to the therapist, however, is like the scalpel to the surgeon. I would no more advocate teaching hypnosis to a layman and saying, "Now that you can open a person's mind, you are a clinical hypnotherapist," than I would show that layman how to use a scalpel and say, "Now you are ready to go off and practice surgery."

I have been using hypnosis extensively in my counseling practice since 1978. In many of the cases to be described in this book, I hypnotized the patients. I hope the case studies will help the reader better comprehend this ancient, still poorly understood and underutilized therapeutic modality.

In terms of current understanding, hypnosis is a difficult phenomenon to analyze—much clearer in certain of its effects than in its basic nature. We have a better grasp of what hypnosis is *not* than of what it *is*. Two common misconceptions are important to eliminate. Hypnosis is not sleep, nor is it a submissive trance in which a person's will is overcome by the will of the hypnotist.

Even the experts cannot unanimously agree on a proper definition except to stipulate that hypnosis is an altered state of awareness. Many will also stipulate that this awareness is characterized (or often characterized) by a heightened ability to concentrate or focus the mind. This description makes it clear that hypnoidal (hypnosis-like) states overtake our minds very often, although we do not recognize them as such.

Imagine a mother and her six-year-old son, Tommy, walking through a shopping mall. As the mother pauses to look into a shop window, the little boy lets go of her hand to pick up a toy he has dropped. For a moment—just a fleeting moment—the mother pays no attention. Then she looks down and Tommy is gone, suddenly vanished among the crowd of shoppers. In that instant, she realizes Tommy is lost, and in that same instant, she begins frantically to look and listen for him.

If she hears someone call out another child's name, she may not even hear it. If her boy is wearing a yellow raincoat, she focuses on that color and may not see— almost certainly will not remember seeing—a boy of the same size passing by in a red raincoat. She need not *consciously* make a decision to watch for yellow and to hear certain sounds above all others; she automatically does so. She is listening for his voice, hoping to hear him call out, "Mommy!" And she is subconsciously hoping to hear someone who knows him—some neighbor or friend who happens to be in the mall—call out his name. She is in an altered—heightened but narrowly focused— state of awareness and alertness for the color yellow and the sound "Mommy" or "Tommy." This is a hypnoidal state that commonly occurs when it will benefit us.

People who feel light-headed or faint at the sight of blood have physiological reactions as if they themselves were bleeding. Likewise, gagging when you see someone vomit, or wincing when you see someone get hurt is an example of hypnoidal reaction in which your digestive or nervous system behaves as if you were injured. In clinical hypnosis, we simply help the patient to marshal and focus this natural ability toward a therapeutic goal.

Since 1978, I have hypnotized thousands of subjects. I will present a very small but, I believe, revealing sampling in the following chapters of this book. It is my hope that in sharing these case studies with you, I will help you understand how I have formulated my convictions regarding soul and spirit as part of every patient, every human being.

Except where otherwise noted, I have disguised the identities of the patients, for confidentiality *must* be respected and protected. In all other details, everything I relate will be factual. I have selected cases that I find to be typical or especially significant and verifiable. I have stated some of my conclusions and will state others in the course of describing patients and incidents. I have also stated emphatically that I do not have "the call of the missionary." I have drawn my conclusions, and I leave it to you, the reader, to draw your own.

PART II

CASE STUDIES

5 ✧ When Anna Was Elizabeth

Until 1986, the concept of reincarnation held no interest for me. I considered it the stuff of fiction, supermarket tabloids, and exotic or primitive religions with no more reality (or relevance in my life) than a belief in leprechauns. Then, in the spring of that year, I received a phone call from a woman whom I will call Anna. She told me she was a nurse and had found my name in the yellow pages of the phone directory. She wanted to begin a weight-reduction program.

I wondered why a practicing nurse would look for a therapist in the phone directory instead of asking a doctor for a referral, and it was not even her own county's directory, for she lived some distance from me. I wondered if perhaps she had some other problem beyond a need to diet and exercise.

But that was all I wondered about. I had no intimation that my subsequent encounters with Anna would change my beliefs, my clinical approach and convictions, my life. When she arrived at my office for our first session, I perceived nothing unusual about this somewhat over-weight but pleasant-looking woman in her mid-thirties who was concerned about her physical fitness and ap-pearance.

Having used hypnosis successfully and often to alter undesirable habit patterns, I used it again in this in-stance to help Anna lose weight. She proved to be an ex-cellent subject. The results were not immediate or dramatic, of course, but they were encouraging. During the next two months, she showed considerable progress toward her goal. But then, quite suddenly and unexpect-edly, she developed right-lower-quadrant abdominal pain and tenderness, and her menses stopped. She asked me if hypnosis could alleviate these symptoms, but I was concerned about what was *causing* the symp-toms. Having worked in emergency medicine for over twelve years, I had occasion to diagnose hundreds of cases of abdominal pain. She could be suffering from an ovarian cyst, colitis, diverticulitis, appendicitis, or per-haps an ectopic pregnancy (wherein the fetus develops not in the uterus but in a Fallopian tube or in the perito-neal cavity). Although she said she was having an active sex life, she dismissed any possibility of pregnancy. Sup-posedly "impossible" pregnancies occur rather often, however, and I was not about to take chances with a patient's health—or life.

I immediately started a diagnostic workup, but the pregnancy test was negative, and the complete blood count (CBC), urinalysis, and electrolytes proved unre-markable. Her symptoms were quickly intensifying; her abdomen was becoming more swollen and tender, and she was getting weaker. Although I insisted that she see her gynecologist immediately, she at first refused, declaring that nothing very serious could be wrong.

Two weeks later, I repeated the blood studies at a different lab, but the results were the same—nothing abnormal. I felt I had to be adamant, and I told her I would not make another appointment with her until she obtained a thorough gynecological evaluation. Reluctantly, she agreed.

On the basis of a first, thorough examination, her gynecologist made a presumptive diagnosis of ectopic pregnancy. While the operating room was being readied for an emergency laparotomy—exploratory abdominal surgery—the doctor sent her to the sonography lab for a confirmation of the diagnosis (or the discovery of an abnormal mass such as a tumor). Fifteen minutes later, the sonography technician called the doctor to tell him no ectopic pregnancy or other masses showed on the sonogram. The operation was canceled, and the patient was sent back to me.

During one of her subsequent sessions with me—five months to the day after her last menstrual flow—Anna was telling me about her mounting though vague, nonspecific feelings of anxiety and depression. Apart from her weight and her distressing abdominal symptoms, she seemed to have some personal problem that she could not or would not put into words and which I could not pinpoint. I put her under hypnosis and instructed her, "Go back now to where your problem started. Go back to where it began."

I was in no way prepared for what was to unfold. In deep trance, she held her right side and began to moan as I questioned her. "Tell me what's happening to you," I said. "What's troubling you, and where and when is this happening."

"Long ago," she replied. "Long ago, not now, not here."

"Where, Anna? When?"

"My name is Elizabeth," she replied, and then her story unfolded.

She spoke of what sounded like a different lifetime in which she was Elizabeth, nineteen years old and in her fifth month of pregnancy. She was in Europe—but she did not say precisely where in Europe and seemed to regard my questions about that as odd—as if I should know something so obvious without asking. As to when, it was centuries ago, but again she was not specific. Her reaction was as if the question were irrelevant, the answer obvious, and her need to recall the scene itself far more important. Her pregnancy had become very difficult, continually painful, and now a priest and a physician were at her bedside. She could hear them talking.

"We must take the baby," the physician said. "We must take it from her or the woman will die."

"No!" the priest said emphatically. "We cannot take life even to save a life. You will not kill the unborn infant. If God wills that the woman die, then she dies."

With that, Anna became visibly weaker, and then a look of peacefulness, serenity came over her face. Suddenly, she was absolutely still. It was as if her pulse and breathing had stopped.

"Anna," I said quickly, "Anna, what is it? What's happening?"

When she did not answer, I realized my mistake. "*Elizabeth*," I said to her, "you must tell me what's happening."

"I've died. I'm floating now. I'm floating up—into a tunnel of light." I had counseled several patients who had undergone near-death experiences, and her account sounded startlingly like theirs—the floating, the rising up into a tunnel or source of light. I suddenly had a very chilling thought—what if this patient goes into this light of death and is not turned back? Am I killing her?

I talked to her soothingly, giving her a healing affirmation that the pain of her previous life—her previous body—had died when that body died and would no longer afflict her. Then I rapidly brought her out of trance.

Most patients tend to recall everything said during hypnosis, but a few do not. Anna is never subsequently aware of what she says during hypnosis. On that occasion, when she came out of trance she exclaimed, "My God! You finally did it, Dr. Jarmon. I feel great. The pain is gone." So was her abdominal swelling, tenderness, and generalized weakness.

Afterward, I sat alone in my office for some time—I am not sure how long—thinking about what I had heard and seen, marveling, trying to puzzle it out, and at the same time experiencing a feeling of deep thankfulness. The marvel of it was not over, as I discovered that evening. She phoned me to tell me excitedly—with understandable relief and happiness that her menstrual flow had returned. I did not know what to make of this and hardly knew what to say. All I could think of in response was to reschedule her next visit for the following week and tell her I was glad for her.

During that next visit, I put her into deep trance and again regressed her—took her back once more to that deathbed scene. Without her consciously realizing it, something in her mind or soul had been awakened or activated, had prepared her to go more deeply and in a more direct way into that life and death she had experienced centuries ago. When she spoke this time, she addressed me as if I were the priest at her bedside.

I decided to play the role of the priest as she expected me to in order to discover where this experience of a previous life would lead. "Elizabeth," I said, "do you understand that God forbids the taking of life? Do you understand why I cannot permit the physician to kill the infant by taking it from you?"

"Yes, Father," she replied.

"Do you have anything you wish to tell me, Elizabeth?"

"No, Father, I have confessed my sins. I am ready to die."

I did not answer for a moment. I hesitated, thinking very hard what might be the best thing to say to her, wondering if perhaps the priest would tell her—had told her—that she might not die, although he knew she would. Or perhaps I should say so now, before letting matters progress any further; perhaps I should give her a quick healing affirmation and bring her out of trance. As I now remember that session with Anna, it seems as if interminable minutes passed while I sat silent and indecisive, but I feel sure only a second or two passed and then her voice interrupted my thoughts.

"Oh, my God," she intoned, "I am heartily sorry. . ."

"Elizabeth," I said. "Elizabeth? Anna?"

" . . . for having offended thee," she continued, "and I detest all my sins because I dread the loss of heaven and the pains of hell, but most of all . . . "

I did not interrupt her again, for I recognized her words—words very familiar to me as a Catholic. They were familiar, but utterly astonishing.

" . . . because they have offended Thee, my God, who art all good and deserving of my love. . ."

She was reciting the Act of Contrition, the prayer a Catholic says at the end of confession or during last rites.

But Anna is Jewish, as are her parents, her husband, her entire family. After bringing her out of trance, I asked her about it.

"Anna, do you know the Act of Contrition?"

"Act of Contrition? No, what kind of act is it?"

I repeated it for her and then asked, "Anna, does it sound familiar to you? It's a Christian prayer."

"No," she said, "I've never heard it before. I'm Jewish, you know."

"Yes, I know," was all I could think to say. What I was saying to myself, however, was "I have a feeling, Bob, we have just begun a journey unlike any we could ever dream up. Hang on tight for the ride."

6 ✧ A Reunion of Ancient Colleagues

My astonishment at Anna's ability to recite a prayer she had never heard in her present life—but had known since childhood in a previous existence several hundred years ago—was amazing, but it was far from the only revelation she was to bestow.

Her weight problem was greatly alleviated during the course of our counseling sessions, and her regression to a previous life as Elizabeth ended all symptoms of ectopic pregnancy. At the same time, her depression and unnamed anxieties melted away. Some current problems troubled her. I did not stop seeing her, for I now wanted to discover anything that might still lie dormant in her mind or soul, anything still waiting to be revealed.

Further exploration could in no way harm her on the contrary, it might help her and most certainly would help me in my future dealing with other patients. She wanted to continue our sessions, and under hypnosis during subsequent visits she described ten more lifetimes!

I still did not know what to make of this and wondered if I might be dealing with multiple-personality disorder—or even simple confabulation. Of course, I did not know then a number of things I know now about people who recall and even (under hypnosis) reexperience episodes from previous lives. One such aspect is that these people often recall past lives that were somehow intertwined with the past lives of acquaintances, colleagues, or relatives existing in the present. A person might recall, for example, that a (present) brother or close friend was known (as an entirely different person) in a past life.

Anna had experienced some lifetimes that were happier or easier or more content than others, and she actually had a favorite. In that life, she had worked in what she described as a "healing temple"—and she was quick to add that I had worked there, too! The temple was adorned with a symbol, a butterfly, and behind the pillared building was a garden with an adjacent pool where the healers went to refresh themselves at the end of the day and have a cup of wine.

The description intrigued me. One detail aroused my suspicion, but only briefly—her mention of the temple's pillars—because my office is attached to my home, which has large pillars at the front. More perplexing was her mention of the garden and pool behind the temple. Behind my home, I have a garden and adjacent pool, but she had never seen them and could not have known about them. She could not identify the time or place of this healing temple (though she was certain she had been there many centuries ago), so there was no way I could try to verify much of what she related. I told none of my colleagues about this unusual case. Most, if not all, of them would probably have laughed.

Several months later while in my local bookstore picking up a book that had been suggested to me by my next past-life patient, I noticed a book lying atop others on a shelf. Out of idle curiosity, I took it down. It was entitled *Many Lives, Many Masters,* by Brian L. Weiss, M.D. The phrase "many lives" caught my attention, and since the author was a doctor, I was curious enough to read the jacket copy on the book: "The true story of a prominent psychiatrist, his young patient, and the past-life therapy that changed their lives." Dr. Weiss was head of the psychiatry department at Mount Sinai Hospital in Miami. I bought the book, and what I read astounded me.

Dr. Weiss and I shared identical experiences and reactions to the accounts of patients under deep trance. The coincidence, however, even if it was nothing more, did not end there. Our fathers had the same names, the same religion, the same age and time of death, the same mode of death. Our mothers-in-law had died of the same disease while we had helped them as well as we could to "pass over" into death. We are the same age. We had never known each other, but we had grown up only five miles apart.

His book is an account of his therapy sessions with a patient named Catherine (a pseudonym to protect her confidentiality) who, like my patient, Anna, worked in a hospital. In deep hypnosis, Catherine—again like Anna—recalled past lives. Eventually, in fact, she dumfounded Dr. Weiss by claiming to have had eighty-six previous lives and by actually recalling, describing in some detail, a full dozen.

Catherine had sought psychiatric therapy because she had been suffering from deepening depression, anxieties, and phobias. Once, when she was very young, she had been pushed into a swimming pool, but that episode did not seem to explain her irrational fear of drowning. The reason for this particular phobia became clear as she recalled one of her previous lives, which had ended with drowning. Similarly, much of her depression and recurrent anxieties could be interpreted in the light of her previous incarnations. In one life, she had been among the thousands of victims of an epidemic; in others, she had experienced abuse, lifelong poverty, and incidents of fear or mistreatment. As Dr. Weiss pointed out, such traumatic experiences, even the less severe ones, affect our mental health and ability to function—"get ground into our psyches," as he aptly expressed it.

But Catherine's mental health improved dramatically as she recalled both the serene and horribly traumatic experiences her soul had undergone in past incarnations. The process seemed to purge her present-life psyche of accumulated burdens. In my own dealings with Anna, I was beginning to speculate that the common modern perception of death is not at all real; that death is not obliteration for all eternity; that the soul survives; and that the realization of this survival can have great therapeutic value.

In the eighth chapter of his book, Dr. Weiss summarized some of his basic conclusions about the type of therapy, and I found myself in total agreement with those conclusions. Pointing out that Catherine's improvement was dramatically rapid without the aide of any medicine, he ascribed the therapeutic progress to "a force apparently much more effective than conventional therapy or modern medicines." This "force," he explained, included remembering and sometimes actually reliving not only severe, dramatic traumas but also the "daily insults to our bodies, minds, and egos"—the unhappiness and misfortunes that in greater or lesser degree assault all human beings.

As he "scanned" Catherine's previous lifetimes and gently probed them with his questions, he had sought the patterns of those insults to the mind and emotions, just as a psychiatrist practicing more conventional therapy seeks patterns while listening to a patient's account of traumatic events and reactions to those events. "The technique," he soon realized, "was similar to reviewing a childhood in conventional therapy, except that the time frame was several *thousand* years, rather than the usual ten or fifteen years."

My own experiences and conclusions in this realm, though more limited at that time, precisely paralleled Dr. Weiss'. In fact, they were identical. But long before I reached the eighth chapter, wherein he presents his conclusions, on page sixty-four in Chapter Five—I had found something even more astonishing in personal terms. At this point, Catherine had been reviewing a lifetime in which she had pierced her foot with some sharp object and had gone to a healing temple to have the resulting infection treated. She went on to describe a bleak and poverty-stricken life in which she aged rapidly and soon died. The vivid recollections seemed to exhaust her, and Dr. Weiss decided to bring her out of hypnosis quickly.

Before he could do so, however, she suddenly declared that someone named Robert Jarrod needed his help. He had no idea who Robert Jarrod might be, and during a subsequent hypnotic session he questioned her about her strange, unexpected statement.

When he asked her who Robert Jarrod was, she replied, "I don't know . . . He may be in another plane, not this one." By this she meant that Robert Jarrod might not be in the lifetime or period between lives that she was then recalling. Catherine added, "Only when he wants, only if he decides to come to me, he will send me a message. He needs your help."[1]

As I read the passage, I was thunderstruck. The mounting coincidences were too many and too great to *be* coincidences. Dr. Weiss had understood Catherine to say "Jarrod"—and perhaps she had—but I wondered if she was saying "Robert Jarmon." I wrote to Dr. Weiss that evening. When he received the letter, he phoned me. Even before he read it, he knew! He said that when he saw my name over the return address on the envelope, he realized that Jarmon was the name his patient was trying to say.

Thus began a series of letters and phone calls. He was planning to come from Florida for a lecture, and we arranged to meet in New York City. Shortly before the meeting took place, I saw Anna again. I had a strong hunch about the connections among the three of us—not just Dr. Weiss and me, but Anna, as well. While she was under trance, I asked if she saw a time when we had been together before.

"Yes," she said, "at the healing temple. Dr. Weiss was the older healer—the senior healer. He had a white beard, long white hair, and wore a long white robe."

I phoned Dr. Weiss and asked if he had ever been regressed to a previous life. He had. In fact, he had seen several lives. At different times he had been a priest, a physician, and a healer. (In this context, a "healer" is a person who combines the functions of physician, priest, and teacher—a concept common to several ancient societies in Asia, Africa, and Europe.) I asked what he knew of his lifetime as a healer.

"Apparently," he said, "I was the senior healer—the chief healer or elder, you might say—in a healing temple. I know that the temple had pillars, and I had a long white beard. My hair was long and white, and I wore a long white robe."

"Did the temple have some sort of symbol?"

"A butterfly. And there was a garden in back of the temple."

"And next to the garden," I said, becoming more and more intrigued, "was there a pool where the healers would bathe and refresh themselves at the end of the day?"

"Yes. There *was*. How did you know?"

"I believe I worked with you there," I said. "It was a long time ago."

When at last we met in New York, Dr. Weiss and I felt like two old and dear friends meeting again after a long separation. Perhaps I should say three old friends—or three former co-workers. Anna, after all, had served at the temple and had described my presence there and Dr. Weiss' as well. I brought her to the meeting in New York. Afterward, she told me she had had a vision as she watched and listened to us talk. Again she saw Dr. Weiss and me back at the garden of the healing temple. The aged healer, Dr. Weiss, was nearing the end of his life, and I was saying to him that it would be difficult to carry on the work without him. He told me not to fret; that the work would continue at a later time; that a future time would come when we would again be working together.

In November, 1992, Dr. Weiss, Dr. Raymond Moody, and I conducted a three-day workshop entitled "The Healing Power of Past-Life Memories." It took place at Edgar Cayce's Association for Research and Enlightenment (A.R.E.) in Virginia Beach, Virginia. Registrants came from Canada, Mexico, and all over the United States. The organizers of the conference wrote to me afterward to say that it was by far one of the most successful programs in the sixty-one-year history of the Association.

I have now counseled hundreds of patients with whom I have conducted past-life therapy. I feel compelled to continue my work in this field and take careful note of the findings as they unfold. Dr. Oliver Wendell Holmes observed that "Man's mind, once stretched by a new idea, never regains its original dimensions." My mind has been stretched, as have the minds of many colleagues and patients. At moments when all this seems too bizarre to be valid, I remind myself that so did the Copernican concept when people first heard or read of it. The "modern" science of that age "knew" the sun rotated around the earth and the earth was the center of the universe—until a new idea stretched the minds of astronomers.

Although Dr. Weiss has broken new ground in this field, so have others, and he is by no means the only physician who has written about healing patients by means of past-life therapy. Other books come to mind: *Coming Back*, by Raymond Moody, M.D., Ph.D.; *Life Between Life*, by Joel Whitten, M.D., Ph.D.; and *Mind Probe Hypnosis*, by Irene Hickman, D.O. I still assess in my own mind what portions of my patients' stories might be true past-life memories, personal allegories, imaginations, or tappings into the cosmic consciousness. Meanwhile, my patients are getting better—at times with incredible speed—and that is what my job is all about.

Sometimes people ask me if this work causes me a conflict of conscience with my Catholicism. I have no problem with that (though my pastor might). I see religion as a means to an end, the end being the attainment of a connection with God to make this life meaningful and ultimately achieve a higher level of oneness with Him. The Church once persecuted and tortured its members who believed in reincarnation or believed that the earth was not the center of the universe. In 1992, it officially changed its tenets on the rotation of the planets. Perhaps a hundred years from now it will re-entertain its view of reincarnation. Meanwhile, I feel obligated to make the most of this brain that God gave me and not to permit my religion to interfere with my spirituality.

7 ✧ The Night Screamer

Gertrude was a short, stocky, pleasant woman in her mid-fifties who came to me in the hope that hypnosis might help her stay with a diet and lose weight. She was my first paying patient for hypnosis therapy, and I was anxious to serve her well. It may be that I had another motive besides the wish to render effective treatment; I needed to prove to myself that I could use hypnosis beneficially. As I was later to see time and again in my practice, weight control is one of the most frustrating of common problems.

I performed a simple, standard induction and gave her post-hypnotic suggestions to the effect that she would enjoy a sensation of her hunger pains eating away her excess fat. When she was out of trance, I asked her how she felt.

"Well, I feel rested," she said. "It's a nice feeling. I don't get much rest."

She had not mentioned this previously. It occurred to me that she might have some problem more serious than an inability to stay on a diet and exercise. I asked her why she got so little rest.

"I don't sleep well," she said. "It's a wonder my husband has stayed with me all these years. I mean, I know I disturb him. I hardly ever sleep through the night. Two or three times a night I wake up, sometimes screaming. I've done it all my adult life."

I questioned her further, trying to help her pinpoint when this traumatic pattern began. She remembered that until she was about eighteen years old, she never had a problem sleeping. I asked her what had been going on in her life at that time.

"I got married when I was eighteen, and I became pregnant very soon."

Gertrude had already told me that she had no children. I asked her what had happened.

"It was terrible," she said. "I wanted that baby so much. We set up a nursery so our child would have a great start in life. We talked and planned for it. It meant a lot to us, especially to me, I guess. Then in the sixth month I miscarried. I just suddenly miscarried."

"That must have been terrible for you," I said.

"I couldn't believe it. Every night for months I'd light a candle and go into the nursery. It sounds crazy, but I wasn't just mourning. I think I was hoping to go in there and find a healthy baby in the crib. I never talked to anyone about it until now. I mean, it does sound crazy. If I still have nightmares now, I don't remember them afterward; but maybe that's why I wake up screaming. Do you think that can be it, Dr. Jarmon?"

"I'm sure it is, Gertrude," I told her. "You're a good hypnotic subject. Would you like me to regress you and end the night screams—put the sleep disturbance to rest?"

"My God, of course! Can you do that?"

Quickly I had her back in hypnotic trance, and I recounted to her the story she had just told me. But in doing so, while speaking to her subconscious mind, I brought the remembered episode to its conclusion. She had never fully felt—come to terms with—the closure of this tragedy.

"That life that once was growing inside you," I said, "was never born. There never was a baby in the nursery. The child never was born, never had to face the pains of this earthly existence and is at peace now. You and your husband have a good, loving life together even though you've had no children. Now your childbearing years are over, and you're going on to the next chapters in life. There's no more need to wake up in the middle of the night. From now on, you'll sleep peacefully and soundly, and you'll wake up each morning refreshed." That entire procedure took no more than two minutes.

I will confess that I was not totally confident of that outcome; after all, she was one of my first hypnosis patients, and my experience at that time was hardly comparable to the experience I have since accumulated. But I was very careful to betray no lack of confidence; on the contrary, I knew I must instill confidence in the patient. Indeed, it worked.

After thirty-seven years of suffering, her problem disappeared. That is, her night-screaming problem abruptly stopped. Weight control turned out to be more difficult, however, a more obstinate problem. I continued to see her for a year with the frustrating results that often hamper weight therapy. During that year, however, her nightly rest was peaceful, and there was no recurrence of the terrified, screaming awakenings.

Then one day she called me to say that the screaming had come back. It happened right after she had undergone general anesthesia for a hysterectomy. A very bright, perceptive person, she asked me precisely the right questions: "Do you think maybe the anesthesia wiped out the post-hypnotic suggestions you gave me? Can you see me again and repeat the hypnosis? Maybe this time the suggestions will stick with me."

I assured her there was no "maybe" about it, and immediately made an appointment for her. It required only one more hypnotic session to end her problem permanently. Her sleep disorder never again returned. This was an example of how powerful a therapeutic tool is regression under hypnosis—whether the regression carries a patient back into a past life, or back only a few years, or back half a lifetime.

8 ✧ Forgotten Injuries

To his neighbors and customers, Carl must have seemed a very normal, solid citizen, a healthy, reasonably content middle-class American of the twentieth century: forty years old, proprietor of a moderately prosperous hardware store, happily married, father of four. He was clean-shaven, dressed casually but neatly, of medium height and build, with a slightly ruddy complexion and sandy colored hair almost hiding a few early wisps of gray. He smiled easily and expressed himself with confidence in a firm, rather deep baritone voice. There would have been no reason to notice him in a crowd.

But anyone who spent much time with him would sooner or later see that something was not quite right. Beneath his normal, healthy appearance, evidently maintained by rigorous self-control, there was a restless mass of fears and idiosyncrasies that occasionally burst through his calm outward manner during moments of stress. When nervous, he trembled, sometimes flailed his limbs, and felt his throat constrict as if he were choking. Any small change in the course of his life was more distressing to him than it would be to an emotionally healthy person.

He sought therapy to obliterate these symptoms and find the cause of his vague feelings of anxiety and depression. An excellent hypnotic subject, he was able to go into deep trance early in our work, and under hypnosis he began to uncover incidents of childhood abuse— physical, emotional, and sexual—of which he had not been consciously aware. He also revealed several past-life scenarios which seemed to explain some of his fears and reactions to stress—particularly the choking and limb flailing. These sessions of hypnotic regression had a clearly cathartic effect. He would envision a past-life experience of being hung, which triggered those reactions, and I would then give him an appropriate healing affirmation before bringing him out of hypnosis.

Afterward, there was no recurrence of his nervous symptoms, and I was satisfied that his therapy was progressing well. All the same, I sensed—and undoubtedly Carl himself sensed—that at least two other, still shrouded aspects of his past remained somehow to be resolved. One of these involved his wife and was a positive rather than negative factor in his outlook on life. He had shared a substantial part of a past existence with her—that is, he had had a relationship with her during one of his (and her) past lives—and now he had a strong sense that he had come into his present existence in order to "help her with something she needs to do in this life."

Hypnotic regression is a marvelously revealing tool of therapy but carries no implication of omniscience. Carl and I never did discover precisely what his wife needs to do in this life that requires his help, and perhaps we never will discover it. Perhaps what she needs—what they both need of each other—is not any single, specific opportunity to help but simply the close bonding and mutual support of their good marriage. Carl's wife has no idea what the "something" might be and no urgency to discover it. If her future holds some ordeal, effort, or accomplishment demanding his help, she knows he will be there. He knows it, too, and that is enough.

But what about that second, still shrouded aspect of his past? Although I could not guess what it might be and had no way of knowing whether it had occurred in his current life or in a previous existence, I felt certain that his subconscious held some memory—a consciously forgotten memory—that must be addressed.

When therapy is going well (and sometimes when it is not going well at all), a rapport grows between therapist and patient. The psychiatrist may detect, or merely suspect, some hidden, unresolved problem, although the stimulus or clue that prompts the suspicion is not always readily apparent. The clue, in fact, may be nothing more definite than a fleeting expression on the face of the patient, a gesture, a manner of speaking, a mild feeling of malaise, or a tendency to make cryptic or seemingly irrelevant remarks. In Carl's case, I tried without success to analyze what clues he might have given me, but I was not surprised when one day he came to his session looking distraught.

At first he volunteered no reason for his obvious distress, but upon questioning, he said that for several days he had been having terrible headaches and severe abdominal pain. Naturally, I began to question him further on the assumption that I might have to refer him to another doctor for treatment of a physical ailment. Then he said that what bothered him even more than his pain was a deep sense that something was about to come out of him, as if he needed to regurgitate something. He had no conscious awareness of what the something might be, and his sense of it was mental rather than physical, involving no feeling of nausea or convulsion.

Then he became somewhat more talkative than usual. He said he had been thinking a lot lately about a vaguely remembered incident that had occurred when he was eleven years old. While riding his bicycle, he had fallen hard and fractured his skull. He did not know why he had been recalling that accident lately, except that his headaches perhaps brought back the memory of the pain of that skull fracture. Suddenly, I realized why I had suspected something unknown was troubling him, as if about to surface. He had indeed given me a clue.

While under hypnosis during previous sessions, he had recalled that fall but remembered himself hitting the street and then being aware only of standing somewhere looking down a steep stairway, like a sudden change of scene in a movie, and I had elicited no explanation when I attempted to probe further.

Now, however, perhaps because his therapeutic progress had at last made it possible, his subconscious was about to provide both patient and psychiatrist with new enlightenment. We were to discover that, in this instance, a trauma inflicted on him in his present life was causing more serious repercussions than anything he had experienced in previous incarnations. Under hypnosis, I asked him to go back to that day when his skull was fractured. The following story came forth.

Once again he was a boy of eleven, and he was riding his bike to a friend's house. He was pedaling fast when the front wheel hit something and turned sharply sideward. He felt himself hurtling through the air, and then he hit the street, hard. He stood up, shaken—bruised, lacerated, and alarmed—*but his skull was not fractured.* His head had not struck the pavement! The bruises and scrapes were painful, however, and he decided to turn back and walk his bicycle home.

When he arrived, he called out to his mother, but heard no response and could not find her downstairs. He then went up to her bedroom, heard her inside—talking softly and moving—and he opened her bedroom door and walked into the room. She was in her bed with a man, not his father but a stranger. Leaping from the bed, the man shouted, "Don't you knock before you come in?"

Thoroughly startled and confused, Carl took several steps backward, retreating from the room, but the man lunged forward. Just as the boy turned around to run downstairs, the man struck his back, pushing him hard. Carl toppled down the steep stairway, hitting his head on the floor below.

Now, almost thirty years later, Carl was reliving the experience under hypnosis, vividly seeing the enraged man pursuing him even after he had fallen. "He's after me," Carl said breathlessly. "He's coming down and I can't move, I can't get away. He's going to kick me—he's kicking me in the stomach, and I can't move!"

I asked him what happened next. Clutching his abdomen and grimacing, he replied, "He's kicking my stomach."

Then, quite abruptly, the expression of pain and fear left Carl's face. "Now I'm going into the light," he said. "It's so peaceful. I see some people—I don't know who they are, it's too bright to make out their faces . . . I want to stay here . . . Now I see a kind, older man . . . He appears and puts his hand on my shoulder. He says I'll have to go back. I tell him I don't want to. He says, 'I know you don't want to, but there's someone you're going to meet who needs you. You'll be all right. You'll make it.'"

I said nothing for a few moments, waiting to see if he

would continue, but he sat there silently. Finally, I asked him what happened next. His only response was to clutch at his abdomen, writhe in pain, and begin weeping. He had gone through enough, and I decided to give him a healing affirmation without further delay. I assured him that he had done the right thing, the only thing he could do, and I reaffirmed that everything would work out happily, as it was meant to be. Bringing him back to the present, I told him gently that the attack, the injuries to his head and stomach, the pain were now many years behind him, and, having brought the long-blocked memory forth at last, he would no longer be troubled by headaches and abdominal pain.

I now understood that his conscious mind had been unable to face the memories of all that had happened *after* his minor bicycle accident—the discovery of his mother with a lover, the vicious attack by the lover, the fall downstairs, the skull fracture when he hit the floor below, the terrible kicks to his abdomen, even his subsequent treatment at a hospital where he had come so close to death. He saw himself going over to the other side, "into the light," only to be turned back because it was not yet his time to die.

Other patients have told me of near-death experiences and their accounts have been eerily similar, all of them agreeing about a sensation of light, or going up and into a place or tunnel of light, and some of them seeing people (or spirits? or angels?) waiting to greet them or turn them back to continue living.

Unable to bear those terrible memories, Carl had totally blocked them out of his consciousness, retaining only the memory of the fractured skull and even altering that memory, blending it with, attributing it to, his fall from the bicycle.

I knew Carl would understand that now as well as I did and would understand, too, the gentle command he had been given not to die because his destiny in life was unfulfilled and, in the words remembered under hypnosis, because "there's someone you're going to meet who needs you." The someone was, of course, his future wife—and for that matter the fruit of their union, their children. A single hypnotic session had uncovered curative insights for my patient and, as so often happens, insights that would help me, as well, in counseling other patients.

It was time to bring Carl out of trance, and I did so after stopping as usual to visualize "the resting place of peace and light." I asked him how he felt.

"Tired," he said, "but okay. The headache's gone. The stomach pain, too."

He was perspiring a little, and he wiped his face and nose with his handkerchief. As he did so, I noticed something I had never before seen in my observations of patients after hypnotic regression.

"Carl," I said, "do you remember everything that happened that day?"

"Yes, I think so," he said. "Everything is clear now."

"Well, do you happen to remember, with everything that happened when you got home and the stranger attacked you—when you fell downstairs, did you get a bloody nose?"

"Yes, come to think of it," he said. "Why do you ask?"

I pointed to his handkerchief. It was splattered with blood.

9 ✧ Comatose but Still Listening

I met Mr. Tarantola during his last month of life; or per haps I should say I encountered him, since he never spoke a word to me or anyone else during that entire time. I first saw him early on the first day of my one-month rotation in the intensive-care unit (I.C.U.) while I was a house officer (medical resident) at Johns Hopkins Hospital. He was a pleasant-looking man of fifty-five, and I was soon to learn that he had a lovely, devoted wife and equally devoted son. Although he had a healthy heart, liver, and kidneys, he had suffered a severe vascular disorder that had demanded surgery if he was not to be permanently incapacitated. It was a delicate and somewhat dangerous surgical procedure, but as far as medical science could determine, it had been entirely successful.

The only problem was that my new patient was in a

coma. When the operation was finished, the effects of the anesthesia wore off, and when it was time for the patient to wake up, he simply did not. That had been a full thirty days before my month of duty in I.C.U. began.

In our multimillion dollar I.C.U., he was hooked up to every appropriate monitoring device. But all the monitors in the world could neither help him open his eyes nor detect why he did not.

Every day, his wife and son drove fifty miles to the hospital and sat at his bedside for an hour or more, talking to him as if he could hear and respond. He gave no sign that he could hear them or was aware of their presence. The medical team at Johns Hopkins, acclaimed for their knowledge and experience, was baffled.

When we residents made our rounds each morning, the report was always close to the same: "blood pressure 125/82 and steady, heart rate 76 and regular, respirations 17 and unlabored." We would discuss the case, exchanging observations and reviewing the records. Sometimes our conversation turned to other matters before we left him. After all, Mr. Tarantola could not care or hear what we were talking about; he was in a deep coma. At times, the talk was about him and entirely serious, and at times the medical students present indulged in gallows humor, those nervous little jokes about suffering and death that relieve or cover up our uneasiness about the fragile, tenuous mortality surrounding us in a hospital setting.

I did not like those moments of gallows humor at a comatose patient's bedside. It was at those times that I pondered and reexamined the admonitions of some of my medical school mentors. They had cautioned us that just because a person is in a coma and may show no response, we must not assume that the patient's senses are totally deactivated and that his mind does not absorb what he may very well be hearing. This hypothesis has been confirmed again and again by patients who, under hypnosis, minutely recall what they heard while totally "unconscious" during surgery—including every word spoken by the surgeons, anesthetist, assistants, and nurses. My final encounter with Mr. Tarantola was one of those experiences that stand out in my mind as demonstrating how much more goes on in this process of life and death than meets the eye.

Day after day, I tended to the laconic man in bed No. 3, and my heart ached as I watched his family dutifully—always hopefully—visiting and chatting. Always they asked the same question, although they knew the answer: "Any change since last night?" Then they would apologize for delaying me even a moment in my rounds and thank me for the attention I was giving to their loved one. I went into medicine to relieve suffering, and often I felt ineffectual and helpless, at times prolonging agony instead of relieving it.

Just once, during the third week of my rotation, we did see something that we interpreted as a glimmer of hope. Whether it was real or only wishful thinking—an imaginary straw eagerly grasped because we had been looking so desperately for that glimmer—there was no way of knowing. It happened on the day when his son came to give him wonderful news. The patient in bed No. 3 was a grandfather—his first grandchild had been born, and mother and baby were fine!

There was no visible reaction, and the son leaned close to his father's face and repeated the announcement. Still there was no change of expression on Mr. Tarantola's face, but a single teardrop rolled from the outer corner of his left eye. Could this be a hint of approaching consciousness and greater things to come, or had a speck of dust simply found its way under his eyelid? There was no further response, no way to elicit any further response, and nothing more to do but hope.

On the last evening of my thirty-day rotation on the

unit, I wrote detailed notes on my patients for the benefit of the resident who would be taking over my cases. It was a depressing evening. My closing notes on Mr. Tarantola looked very much like the closing notes the previous doctor had turned over to me a month ago.

I sat there thinking about what Mrs. Tarantola had told me about her husband. He was a very proud, strong-willed man, accustomed to being independent and self-reliant. He had expressed anger at the disorder that had brought him into the hospital, and he was appalled by the probability that he would be at least partially dependent on the ministrations of others for a long time to come. The dangerous aspect of the surgical procedure had not dismayed him in the least, and he had approached it with an "all or nothing" attitude. "Either I'm going to be whole again," he had told her, "or I'm not going to be around."

But he was not going to be whole again—at least in his interpretation of whole—for some time, if ever. The physicians had discussed the gravity of his case and the need for long-term recuperation on a number of occasions, perhaps during surgery and certainly at his bedside in the intensive-care unit while he remained comatose. Had Mr. Tarantola been listening all that time, absorbing every word, slowly coming to a decision that he would not tolerate what he called "a vegetable existence?"

Essentially, he was a fighter, the kind of person who summons previously untapped reserves of strength to fight off death, and this could in some measure explain why his blood pressure, heart rate, respiration—all his life signs—had returned to and remained at such promising levels while he remained mysteriously comatose. But he was also a person who could face and deliberately choose death in favor of a dependent life. Perhaps he had been listening attentively all this time, slowly approaching a decision.

The end of my thirty days had come, and I decided I must have a talk with Mr. Tarantola. I had to disregard the possibility that he could not hear me. I felt certain he could and that I must try somehow one last time to bring him out of his coma. I felt that the probability of success was small and the decision entirely his, not susceptible to any influence I might try to exert. But I had to at least try. I pulled a chair up to his bedside and drew the curtain closed so that we could have a private chat. More honestly, I didn't want the nurses to see me having an intense, one-way discussion with a comatose patient.

"Mr. Tarantola," I said, "this is Dr. Jarmon. I've been taking care of you for the last month. The nursing staff and the other doctors have been doing all they can to get you better. I think you can pull out of this if you really want to, but I don't think you've been trying hard. Your family has been here every day, visiting you, and you know how much they care about you and want you home with them. Don't you think it's time you made a decision? We're doing all we can, but it's up to you. You can work with us to help you get better or you can stop breaking your family's hearts by giving them false hope. It's a big decision, a terrible decision, and you mustn't make it hastily, but I think you *have* been making it, and you'll come out of this if you want to—but only if you want to."

I watched closely for the slightest sign of response. There was none. I decided to continue:

"Mr. Tarantola, your condition hasn't changed at all in sixty days, and another doctor will be taking over your case tomorrow. So I'd like to know your answer today. I'm going to see another patient now, but I'll be back in about fifteen minutes. I'm going to look for your decision then. I'm going to hope you've decided to come back to us. Now, try to blink if you've heard and understood what I've been telling you."

I looked at his face as closely as I ever studied anything in my life, wanting desperately to see him blink or perhaps even open his eyes. I thought I saw an eyelid move, but I could not be sure.

I threw open the curtain and proceeded to my other duties, wondering whether I had just helped a fellow human being, whether I had functioned as a healer or an idiot. No more than three minutes later, the alarm bells sounded on his vital-function monitors. The nurse shouted to me that the man in bed No. 3 was in cardiopulmonary arrest. We tried long and hard to resuscitate him to no avail. His soul had left his body. Mr. Tarantola had made his decision.

10 ✧ Claustrophobic Since Birth

B ack in the late 1950s and early 1960s, there was a teacher of clinical hypnosis who put great emphasis on the precept that traumatic memories lie deeply buried within every mind and that the act of disinterring these memories—bringing them forth and, thus, clarifying their effects on the psyche—often dissipates or dislodges otherwise intractable neuroses, fears, and other psychiatric problems.

Certainly this was not a new hypothesis; its ramifications were clear to see in Freudian psychoanalysis. But this particular practitioner was unusually emphatic concerning the value of *hypnotically* exhumed memories as a speedy therapeutic avenue. I did not study under him but merely heard about his approach from a colleague. I have had to find out for myself how right he was.

When skeptical students expressed doubt that the subconscious mind can retain extremely early images and perceptions—memories of infancy, for example— he replied that he could remember his own birth and had known others who remembered details of their entry into conscious life. Such claims bring up an intriguing question. A person who retains that particular and astonishing image may *think* he actually remembers it, but is he perhaps merely remembering descriptions of it heard during childhood? Is he mistaking what he heard from family members long ago for the actual experience of the event? Sometimes, this is no doubt the case. With or without the aid of hypnosis, this is a viable explanation in some cases.

On the other hand, I have seen cases that defy that easy explanation and can be interpreted only as real memories of personal experience, not memories of hearsay. We have barely begun to explore the enigmatic recesses of subconscious memory.

Roger was a tall, thin, clean-cut college freshman whose manner was lighthearted and relaxed—that is, usually but not always. His father had called me to make an appointment because of concern about his son's occasional, inexplicable bouts of claustrophobia. All his life, Roger had exhibited a mild fear—little more than nervousness—when confined in small, enclosed places. As he matured, the fear had increased, and now the claustrophobic episodes were becoming more frequent yet without any obvious pattern.

His fear seemed to be selective; that is, only certain types of enclosed situations troubled him. He could step into a small but empty elevator or a walk-in closet without great trepidation. In contrast, he sometimes felt almost terrified in a crowded elevator, had difficulty making his way through any narrow passage between buildings, disliked riding in small cars, could not force himself to squeeze past throngs of people in a school corridor or airport, and felt a sensation of panic in narrow doorways or if people or objects pressed against him. Sometimes he even seemed to dislike being hugged.

During our first two sessions, Roger and I explored the nature of his problem but could not come to any conclusion about its cause. With the aid of hypnosis, I tried to provide him with some degree of desensitization and behavior modification, a conventional approach utilizing post-hypnotic suggestion. The results were unimpressive. In conversation with him, I endeavored to discover whether college life might in any way be exacerbating his problem. Perhaps subconsciously he felt daunted by college and had a sublimated impulse to quit, even though he was doing well both academically and socially. But that did not seem to be so, and in fact that path of exploration led nowhere.

During our third session, I guided Roger into a deeper level of hypnotic trance, which was quite easy because he was a relaxed, cooperative subject. Rather quickly, he went into a deep hypnotic state, and I asked him to go back in his mind to where the problem first began. After a few moments of silence, he began to speak in a whispering but intense voice, obviously reliving an experience:

"Cramped—it's cramped. Walls . . . pushing in on me. I'm all hunched over . . . can't get out, no place to go. I can see a little opening, a light. Water all around me . . . The walls are pushing at me—pushing me toward the light. I want to kick. I'm kicking at it. I can't stand this pressure on me! There are people—people on the outside of where I am. They're afraid, too . . . "

On the face of my patient I could see the anxiety he was describing. He hunched over in his chair with his arms crossed, up against his chest, his fists clenching and unclenching, his head lowered toward his knees, and then he straightened somewhat, and his legs kicked spasmodically. He was reliving some extremely traumatic experience and the fear that had accompanied it.

This is a startling but encouraging therapeutic sign. This abreaction, or delayed reaction, to a past, emotionally charged event can set the stage for a therapist's healing affirmation, which can enable the patient to relegate that event to its proper historical perspective. Roger had momentarily fallen silent, and I encouraged him to take up the account again:

"Go on. Tell it. Let it out. What happens now?"

"A gush of water. Something breaking through . . . It's over."

"Now what's happening?"

"Nothing . . . " As Roger said that single word, "nothing," his kicking stopped, he raised his head, and he leaned back in his chair, motionless, and relaxed.

"Nothing? What do you see or feel now?"

"A baby. All I see is a baby lying there on a table. Not moving."

"Is the baby all right? Is it moving? Is the baby breathing?"

"No."

"Is there something more? What's happening now? What do you see next?"

"I . . . I'm floating up . . . away from the baby. I'm going . . . into a tunnel of light."

By the time I worked with Roger, I had treated some twenty patients who had undergone and recalled near-death experiences—or *NDEs,* as we have come to call these recollected experiences—and suddenly Roger was sounding very typical. Most of these survivors had recalled seeing a figure who spoke to them, directing them to return to their bodies—that is, to life. But so far, Roger had said nothing about such a figure or about being turned back.

"Do you see something or someone in the tunnel of light?" I asked.

"No. Nothing. Just the light . . . and down there—the baby. A baby on a table."

I was perplexed, if not a little uneasy. I could accept, even welcome, a patient's exhumed vision of a long-forgotten birth trauma and near-death experience; for I now realized that Roger had been reliving his own birth. But he was also reexperiencing his own soul's departure from the newborn infant's body, its departure without any turning back. If the soul had not returned—if Roger's *life* force had not returned—who was this person in my office, reliving the throes of death? Perhaps the answer was that the baby, Roger himself, had not quite expired and had possessed such a strong will to live that it had returned of its own volition, without the need of being turned back from the tunnel of light.

"Look again, Roger," I urged him. "What now? What do you see next?"

"The baby. The baby is moving again. The baby—kicking and screaming . . . and a doctor is leaning over. More people . . . masks and caps . . . surgical gowns . . . people moving . . . baby moving . . . "

It was time to offer a healing affirmation. I told him that he had, indeed, seen a time in the past, the time of his birth, when a tightly enclosed space—the birth canal—had indeed been a threat to his existence; but that whatever caused the problem, whatever the emergency had been, the experience had long ago and safely passed, and the cause of his fear was gone forever. There was no longer a need to be afraid of enclosed places.

Upon bringing him out of trance, I was mildly surprised to learn that he remembered nothing of what he had undergone only moments before; he recalled not a word of what he had said and not an inkling of what he had felt in trance. He asked what had happened, and I told him—in a general way, without dwelling on details, because I was not sure how he would react to it.

I was further surprised to find that he did not immediately grasp the significance of the scene he had revived: being hunched over, the walls pushing in on him, the water all around, and the opening of light. I had assumed that he would immediately realize he had reexperienced the view from the birth canal and a traumatic birth whose complications had almost brought him forth stillborn. But he did not.

"Well," I asked, "how do you feel?"

"Okay. A little strange but okay."

"Roger, when you were born—when your mother gave birth to you—were there any complications?"

"Complications? No, none that I know of. Why?"

"Because that would explain what you just recalled in hypnosis. You seemed to be remembering your own birth. Don't you think so?"

"I was? I mean, I don't know. It sounds that way, doesn't it? But I don't know. If my Mom had a tough time delivering me, she never said anything about it to me. Dad didn't either. If that's so, they would have told me—or talked about it anyway, wouldn't they?"

"Well, maybe they thought it would bother you. No need to worry about it now. Let's get back to what's going on with you here and now. You're going back to school tonight, aren't you?"

He was but would be on vacation at the end of the week. For the time being, at least, I decided not to tell him about his description of floating above the baby's body and going into the tunnel of light. He had enough to think about, and there was no need to dwell on anything other than the healing affirmation I had given him. I felt confident that he would now be able to conquer his claustrophobia. Better still, it would no longer afflict him—because he would see it as a discardable, no longer appropriate reaction, like a uselessly repeated reflex long after the stimulus that triggered the reflex has ceased. We made an appointment for the following week, and I instructed him to test for himself the healing process—to find out how well he was coming along by deliberately but safely putting himself into an environment that previously would have made him feel fearful.

"How do I do that?" he asked.

"Well, for instance, try walking through a narrow space between school buildings, or step into the school corridor between classes or the entrance to the school cafeteria when it's mobbed at lunchtime. You don't have to put yourself through an ordeal. If you feel uncomfortable, just back out, and we'll try it again later. If you have any problems, call me. Otherwise, we'll get together next week and talk about your progress."

The following week, he arrived a little before his appointed time to tell me jubilantly that he had tested himself with complete success. In perfect comfort, he had tried everything I had suggested and had also stepped aboard a crowded elevator. "The only thing that bothered me was the heavy perfume the physics instructor wears—I don't know how her husband can stand it!"

We repeated the hypnotic regression and healing affirmations of the previous week, but I did not question him again about whether his mother had experienced great difficulty during his birth. If that were the case, evidently his family simply never mentioned it, and I doubted that he would ask them unless I instructed him. I decided to drop the subject until I could discuss it with his parents.

A few days later, I called his mother to ask how Roger was doing. "Great!" she said. "Splendidly!" His claustrophobia simply seemed to have vanished. I asked her if there had been any complications during his delivery.

"What?" she said in a startled voice. "Why, yes. Actually, there was. I went through very long labor, and then, when the time came, I seemed to be delivering a still-born infant. My water didn't break until almost the last minute, and nothing went right. He was limp and he didn't breathe. The doctors tried to get him breathing. I'd had a fairly normal pregnancy, and there weren't any signs of trouble until the time came, and then he just seemed to die before they could get him out.

"They tried to get him breathing for a long time—I don't really know how long—and just when they gave up hope, he suddenly screamed and started breathing, and they never even found out what the problem was. Once he started breathing, he was perfectly all right, and he's never had any physical problems, just the ordinary things that kids get like colds and chicken pox. But, God, what a close call that was. Roger doesn't even know it happened. We never told him about it. We thought it might worry him—you know, make him wonder if he was all right. Or maybe he'd feel guilty that I had such a hard time with him—the pain and the scare. You know how kids get guilty feelings about all sorts of crazy things. But what in the world made you ask? Did my husband mention it? It's always been kind of a secret between us."

I told her, and she was astonished, of course. She did not know what to make of my therapeutic procedure, but she and her husband were vastly relieved that their son's problem was gone at last. Naturally, Roger himself was even happier, and still is. The claustrophobic sensations have never returned. Soon after my conversation with his mother, she told him in detail about his difficult birth. He concluded that the memory of it must, indeed, have lain dormant in his subconscious all these years, one more proof of the untapped power of the mind, and he was glad to have it brought forth and rendered harm-less.

For my part, I always feel very good about such happy

endings, but sometimes I still wonder about his account of leaving his infant body, floating above the stillborn baby, seeing it, seeing the doctors work frantically over it, seeing it come alive again—yet without any memory of being turned back from the tunnel of light, without any memory of returning to his body. That was not at all like the other near-death experiences with which I had become familiar. Had it truly been a near-death experience? Or is it possible that the soul of the fetus departed at birth, never turning back, and another soul, watching and ready, entered the lifeless infant, giving it life anew?

11 ✦ Help from an Old Friend

As a rule, time in my consultation room is devoted strictly to patients in need of therapy, but there have been exceptions. On one such occasion, a man I will call Joe made an appointment for no more urgent reason than to discuss my views about reincarnation, or so he and I both thought. As a consequence, quite unforeseen, he was able to help an old man deal tranquilly with the prospect of death. Or perhaps it would be more accurate to say that his long-dead grandfather helped the old man.

At the time of our meeting, Joe was forty years old, a successful litigation attorney, husky, well-spoken, happily married, the father of two children. Some twenty years earlier, while studying comparative religion in college, he had become interested in the concept of reincarnation. On what I might call an intuitive level, it seemed to him to ring true, but his interest had been mild, more or less sporadic, and he had never explored the possibility of his own past lives.

Then, quite recently, a friend had given him a copy of *Many Lives, Many Masters*, the book in which Dr. Brian Weiss writes of his psychotherapeutic encounters with a patient's past lives (see Chapter Six). Fascinated by the accounts, he contacted the author's office in Miami and asked to be referred to an appropriate psychiatrist in New Jersey—appropriate meaning a psychiatrist who would be prepared to discuss reincarnation without scoffing. He was given my name and location and immediately called me. He told me how long he had been interested in the subject and added that although he had no problems requiring counseling, he felt strongly that he was meant to pursue his old interest again at this time.

Normally, I do not take patients (actually, they would not be patients but merely clients) who are simply curious about past lives. But sometimes I seem to hear an inner voice that tells me to ignore some rule or depart from custom in some way. I have learned to listen to that inner voice, though probably not as consistently or attentively as I should. This was one of those times, and I decided to obey the impulse that told me insistently, "See this one."

Accompanied by his wife, Joe arrived a few minutes early and read some of my office literature while waiting for me. After letting him wait briefly, I brought him into my consultation room and reviewed his life history and current situation. Although I have yet to find anything perfect in this world—certainly not the human psyche— I found myself agreeing that nothing in Joe's life indicated the need for therapy. There was only one unhappy situation bothering him, and it was not his own. An eighty-year-old gentleman named Sal, who had been working for him for many years, was rapidly showing the signs of age that precede the end of a long life. Sal felt that he had, at most, a few years left and had become extremely despondent at the prospect of impending death.

Sal and Joe's grandfather, Vincent, had emigrated from Italy together as young boys, had grown up together in New Jersey, had weathered the Great Depression together, and had served in the army together. They had been the closest of friends, and Vincent's death in the 1960s was a very hard blow for Sal.

Before he died, Vincent had asked Sal to look after his grandson Joey and had asked Joe, in turn, to look after Sal. Joe had always done that to the best of his ability, but now he could find no way to give Sal hope or consolation in facing old age and the end of his life.

Sal's health was failing steadily, and he was becoming acutely depressed. Unfortunately, he was the kind of person who scoffed at psychotherapy and would never consider seeing a counselor. Unlike Vincent, he had chosen to remain in the army when World War II ended and had made a career of soldiering. As a retired army man, he regarded himself as tough and cynical, too worldly wise to be taken in by "shrinks." He had no more use for religion than for psychiatry, never having shared his friend Vincent's spiritual convictions, and with his life coming to a close he felt the hopelessness and isolation of the atheist who has "no invisible means of support." Thus, Joe could find no way or words to comfort his beloved grandfather's old friend.

After discussing this and other matters with me for some time, Joe mentioned that he had practiced self-hypnosis and meditation, and he suggested that I hypnotize him in order to see if regression might lead to any interesting discoveries. We went back through his childhood, and along the way he recalled in more detail conversations with the grandfather about watching over Sal who was not, in Vincent's estimation, quite as self-sufficient as he wished to appear.

Stage by stage, Joe's mind under hypnosis took him back through puberty, into early childhood, into infancy, and then before entry into his present life, to a resting place of peaceful floating and light. Abruptly, he regressed still farther, his mind leaping from that resting place to another life, the life of a soldier of ancient Rome. A good friend from his present lifetime was with him there, too, as a comrade in arms. Together they fought for Rome, and both died by the sword while relatively young.

When he stopped speaking, I brought him forward again in time, but as I did so, he interrupted to describe a new vision. His grandfather appeared and told Joe he was still a warrior and would be a warrior but of a different kind, without resort to force or violence; that he would do better now to become a healer of some sort, a solver of people's problems. It occurred to me that this description could fit his current role as an attorney, though I was also reminded of a friend of mine who had quit the practice of law because he had disliked being a "hired gun" for his clients.

Then something else occurred to me. I asked if his grandfather did not also have some message for his old friend Sal—something that might comfort the man at this unhappy period of his waning life. Joe sat silently for a few seconds and then began to describe another vision, a scene from his grandfather's youth.

Vincent and Sal were young men, walking in a park late at night. Sal was telling his friend of a family vendetta that he had thought was left behind in Italy—until he discovered that immigrants had brought the hatred with them across the ocean. Sal's life had been threatened, and the threat was of a kind to be taken seriously.

Vincent, who was normally not a man of violence but was a man of unshakable loyalty, said he would take care of the situation. No, Sal told him, he must not; this was something he would have to do for himself. He was grateful to his friend but adamant, and he swore Vincent to secrecy.

"What happened?" I asked. "Did Sal carry on the vendetta? Was anyone hurt?" But Joe knew nothing more about it. There were no further visions or recollections.

When I brought him out of his deep trance, he remembered everything he had told me. I asked if Vincent or Sal had ever mentioned that incident. No, he had never known anything about it, had never even been aware that Sal had any enemies.

"Joe," I said, "if it really happened the way you visualized it and no one but your grandfather and Sal ever knew about it, this might be just what Sal needs to hear. Don't you see? A demonstration to him that something does exist beyond the grave could be a source of comfort."

If so, Joe agreed, it could be a wonderful solution, a sort of spiritual tonic for Sal, but perhaps it was all just a product of wishful thinking. He thanked me and said he would keep in touch. Three days later, he phoned.

"Just wanted you to know how good I've been feeling. I really needed to deal with this reincarnation concept. I seem to have a different perspective now, but I have something more important I want to tell you about. I had a talk with Sal. I didn't tell him I went to a psychiatrist— that would have just put him off. I told him I'd had a really strange dream, and then I described the vision I had in your office, about Grandpa and Sal walking in the park. You should have seen his face when I came to the part about the vendetta. He said to me, 'How could you dream that? We never told anybody.' 'Well,' I told him, 'it was in my subconscious.' 'It couldn't come from your subconscious,' he says, 'because you never knew about it, so it was never in your subconscious in the first place.'

"I guess I was just as surprised as he was. So I asked him, 'Then it's true?' 'Yeah,' he says, 'it's true. I just don't understand it.' He didn't seem to want to talk about it any more. He went for a walk and didn't come back for quite a while. Then he just sat around all evening, looking into space. Maybe he was just thinking about old times, but I don't think so. I think it did him good. I'll watch him and let you know how he acts."

I heard nothing more for a couple of months, and then Joe called me again to let me know everything was fine. Sal's health was still deteriorating, but his troubled expression was gone—had been gone ever since their conversation about Joe's grandfather. He seemed at peace with himself and the world.

Sal is still alive but probably not for long, and I doubt that I will ever have a chance to meet him. No matter. Perhaps fate used this office and his friend Joe to give him what he sorely needed. Sal was shown that a precious friendship had not ended with death but, more importantly, that *existence* does not end with death.

12 ✧ Doing Penance

Angela was a patient I had been seeing intermittently for about three years. Initially, she had come to me for help in breaking the smoking habit. She was a middle-aged woman, quiet, trusting, and pleasant, and after a single session she had no difficulty in putting her nicotine addiction behind her.

For several months afterward, she made appointments every two weeks or so, as she could afford them, to get help in losing weight and to talk about a more distressing worry. Her family life had never been entirely happy. Her husband was a good enough sort but not very considerate or attentive. Three of her children had somehow failed to acquire a healthy appreciation of the work ethic. But her deepest concern was about her fourth, the eldest, Maria, a wonderful person who had always been a source of pride and happiness but whose health had been a torment.

Maria had been born with a congenital defect in her renal system and now, at the age of thirty-five, was beginning what would probably be the last year of her life unless she could obtain a kidney transplant. With the deterioration that had already occurred, she was no longer considered a prime candidate for a transplant. Angela was visibly distressed but seemed to accept her lot in life as God's will and was timid about any kind of introspection that might, in her view, amount to questioning that will. When I attempted to probe deeper into her psyche, she stopped coming to me for counseling.

Then one day she phoned again and asked if she could see me that same day. She sounded almost frantic. Her daughter, Maria, who was living alone in California, had taken a turn for the worse. Angela was going to fly out early the next morning to see her. It was after two o'clock when I received her call, and my time was booked solid with patients for the rest of the afternoon and, in fact, most of the evening. By unhappy coincidence, several of those patients needed counseling almost as urgently as Maria did. I told her I was deeply sorry that I had no openings that day but would try to work something out and call her as soon as possible. Then I looked again at my appointment ledger and case notes, pondering which patient would be least distressed by a cancellation.

I had not yet made up my mind when, a few minutes later, my 4 P.M. patient called to say that because a heavy rainstorm had begun, she was afraid to drive to my office and would like to postpone her appointment. I called Angela. She must have been sitting by the phone waiting, because she answered at the first ring. She would be at my office at four.

Shortly before she was due to arrive, my telephone

rang again. It was a friend of mine, Jim, a Roman Catholic priest from Pennsylvania. He had driven in for the day
to visit a colleague at the local rectory. Jim had lately
been struggling with feelings of isolation and frustration—a not uncommon occupational hazard. Today he
was feeling especially depressed. He was at an age when
many priests have their own parishes. Although he was
a kind, gentle, hard-working man, he was becoming resentful, even bitter, over what he regarded as the casual
and callous treatment by the diocese that had passed
over his requests to become a pastor.

Two months earlier, instead of giving him the parish
that the grapevine had told him he would finally get, they
had reassigned him from the church where he was as-
sisting to a pastoral-care ministry. Now, over the phone,
he was releasing some of his anger by confiding in me,
just as any patient might in talking to a psychiatrist.

"You know, Bob," he said, "It really rubs salt into the
wound, giving me this station. It isn't that I don't want to
help these people—I know they need help—but that isn't
what I feel my calling is. The personnel office doesn't
even consider the needs of the priest. We're people, too.
They don't even seem to care about my health. They
know I've got some physical ailments, and here they're
giving me a job with no support, no backup. I'm on call
twenty-four hours a day, working maybe sixteen hours
at a clip and getting complaints that I'm not seeing everybody who asks for the priest. It's easy enough for any
priest to remind himself about praying for guidance and
strength, but I tell you, Bob, this time I feel like I just can't
handle the job."

I tried to think of something comforting to say, but all
I could muster was, "I understand how you feel, I really
do, but isn't it gratifying to work with people who are really looking to the Church for comfort—maybe for the
first time in their lives? Think about the feeling of accom-

plishment you'll have. Doesn't that help some?"

"Not right now," he said. "Sure these people need someone, but why me? I'm getting to understand better and better how Job felt. These people want me to give to them—give and give—and this is a terrible thing for a priest to say, but I'm *tired* of giving. I need to get as well as give. I need it just as much as they do. What I want to know is, when do *I* get?"

A question like that almost defies an answer. How does one respond to a rhetorical question that amounts to a cry for help? A glib reply is no help at all. I hesitated, and Jim did an uncharacteristic thing. He just said, "Well, thanks for listening," and hung up.

At least for the present, there was nothing I could do, no supportive measures I could implement, and when Angela arrived, I made a conscious effort to put Jim out of my mind and concentrate my attention intensely on her problems and hers alone. She began by telling me that her daughter Maria's condition was declining fast and she might not live until Christmas.

"Why is this happening to us?" she said. I've tried to be a good person, a good wife and mother. I pray to Saint Anthony, but I never get any answers. If my patron saint can't help me and God won't, what's left? I pray, and Maria just gets sicker."

Another rhetorical question amounting to an anguished cry for help, and again I had no answer. I had nothing else to offer.

"Angela," I said, "I don't have any more answers than you do. These things are beyond our comprehension, and we have to ask for help from a greater power—ask and keep asking, if need be. If we don't seem to be getting any answers, maybe we need to try asking in a different way. While you're here, why don't we try some hypnotic relaxation and meditation and turn all of these questions over to your guardian angel?"

Does that sound like strange guidance from a counselor trained in medical science? I think not in a case like this. Given Angela's strong religious background, I hoped that an act of faith might give her some enlightenment or at least support. I cannot pretend I was totally confident, but it was worth a try.

She quickly slipped into the trance state, and before I could offer further suggestions or ask any questions, she grimaced, then looked puzzled, then pained, then relaxed again in deep repose. After a moment she smiled fleetingly and began to sob, "My God," she cried, "that's why. Dear God, I'm sorry, I'm so sorry!"

My curiosity rivaled my surprise and relief. "Angela," I said, "tell me. What is it? What's why? What is it you see?"

"The abortion," she sobbed, "the abortion. Of course, the abortion. How could I be so stupid? Why didn't I understand? It was the abortion. Oh, dear God, forgive me."

"The abortion? Tell me about it, Angela. Tell me about the abortion."

"It was forty years ago—three months before our wedding. Our families were Catholic, and I was eighteen and pregnant. We just couldn't tell them. We were so scared. We just didn't know what else to do. What a terrible decision—it was just as bad for him. My God, how we've regretted it. Forty years and we've never even talked about it, not once. My God, forgive me. I've never told another living soul."

Realizing what her belief system was telling her, I replied, "Yes, Angela, but now you've paid that debt, paid it over and over all these years. You've paid a debt of suffering for the sin, but you've suffered enough, and now that you understand it, you can be at peace with yourself."

After coming out of trance, she had no difficulty talking about it to me, the first person she had ever told. It was as if her shame had at last been lifted, as if she had been chained by secrecy and was now released.

"You know, Doctor," she said, "I've done my best to be a good Catholic ever since then, and I've raised my children that way. I've made every sacrifice to God and Saint Anthony that I could think of, but there's one thing I haven't done, the most important thing, a part of the debt I *haven't* paid. I never confessed that abortion to a priest. My greatest sin and I never confessed it. Every time I went to communion, I went with sin in my soul."

Answers were beginning to come to me as well as to Angela. "Would you like to receive the sacrament of confession before you see your daughter tomorrow?" I asked. "Yes. Yes, but the plane—there's no time."

I picked up the phone and dialed the rectory where Jim was visiting. "Father Jim," I said, "I know how much you've been giving, but I need a favor and I'm going to ask you to give again. I need you for an ecclesiastical consultation with a patient of mine who needs confession. She needs it right now."

"Sure," he said. "Why not? Send her over."

When Angela returned from California, she called me.

"That Father Jim is wonderful. We talked for almost an hour. I don't know how to thank you for sending me to him. At the end he said he had no penance to give me— I'd been doing my penance for the last forty years. I feel so relieved now, I can't explain it. It's, well, a peaceful feeling where a burden was. Whatever happens to Maria, I know it's God's will, but you know, I have a good feeling about the future. You can call it faith or whatever, but it's just a good feeling."

Several months later, in mid December, Jim called me.

"Bob, I wanted you to be one of the first to hear the news. I'm getting a parish. It's not very big and it's poor— perfect for me. Lots of potential for some good solid work. Just what I was hoping for. And I got a beautiful note from the bishop, would you believe that? He said he knows how hard I worked at my last assignment; he said I left a wonderful legacy of good feelings about what the Church can do for the people."

Jim went on to say that his perspective on his counseling ministry assignment had changed after his talk with the woman I had sent to him. "I think you sent her over as much to heal me as to heal her," he said.

I had.

A few days before Christmas, I was counseling a patient who was struggling through holiday depression. There was no way for him to know it, but I myself was feeling despondent. That Christmas season was a very sad one for me. During the same week when Angela and Jim had sought my help, my mother had died, and this would be my first Christmas without a parent. Just as the patient was leaving, the telephone rang. It was Angela.

"Dr. Jarmon," she said, "a miracle has happened— Maria got her kidney transplant! This is going to be the best Christmas of our lives. Do you believe in miracles? I hope so. Somehow, I think you had more to do with this than you realize, and I want to thank you. I can't thank you enough. God bless you, Dr. Jarmon, and have a merry Christmas."

Perhaps there is something to this power of angels and saints. At the moment, I had an urge to say, "Thanks, Saint Anthony, I needed that." Do I believe in miracles? As Anwar Sadat once said, "These days, if you don't believe in miracles, you're not a realist."

13 ✧ NDE—Eavesdropper

Occasionally, someone comes to me for help with a seemingly simple problem and unexpectedly reveals a quite different and deeper concern or an experience that has changed the patient's life. My case files include more than two dozen patients who have had near-death experiences (NDEs). Some patients suppressed these experiences, erased them from conscious memory, so that the phenomenon came to light only in the course of hypnosis for other problems. I have also had patients who consciously remembered it all but never spoke of it for fear of being thought insane.

A near-death experience, in this context, does not merely mean almost dying. It means having the actual, though brief, experience of death, passing from life to the other side, or afterlife, and then returning. It is esti-

mated that perhaps eight million people in this country
have experienced this, and it can have strong afteref-
fects.

A case in point was a man I shall call Harry, a phone
company executive in his early fifties who came to me
for support in breaking the smoking habit. During the
first few minutes of our first session, it became obvious
that he was resisting my counseling—to say nothing of
hypnotic induction. Quite often, a smoker asks for help
without genuinely wanting it; what such a patient really
consciously and/or subconsciously wants is a quick failure of therapy. Without any feeling of guilt, he can then
tell himself, his family, and anyone else who cares that
he really did try—even went to a hypnotist—but his case
is hopeless, the addiction too strong and long-estab-
lished. How easy it is then to give up the effort instead of
the nicotine, and light up while shrugging off the last
vestige of responsibility.

I suspected that Harry was that kind of self-vindicat-
ing smoker, and I suggested to him that perhaps he was
not fully cooperative because he was not yet ready to
give up cigarettes.

"No, Doc," he said, "it's not that, believe me. I'm ready
to quit, all right. I've gotten to the point where I don't
even *like* cigarettes, and I know what they're doing to me.
So believe me, it's not that. It's not you. I mean, not you
personally. It's just, well, it's a little embarrassing to tell
you this, but I guess I've got to say it, got to clear the air,
you know? The fact is, I'm sorry, Doc, but I don't much
like doctors. I guess I just don't trust them—not any of
them."

"Did something happen to make you feel that way?" I
asked. "Did you have a bad experience?"

"Well, I had an operation once, and it didn't go too
well. Look, I know it's stupid to generalize, and you're not
a surgeon, you're a psychiatrist, but I don't think I'll ever

feel really confident with a physician again. I guess you could say I'm a little scared of them. Do I want to quit smoking? Well, I came here, didn't I? I *hate* going to doctors. The trouble is, now I'm here, I can't seem to relax and let you help me."

"I think you should tell me what happened," I said. "Tell me about the operation. If that's a block, we need to clear it away so you *can* let me help you."

Hesitantly at first, he related the following story. He had gone into the hospital for a simple hernia repair. His wife had accompanied him and was sitting in a waiting room. They had both been assured the surgery would be simple and relatively fast, and she could see him after he was brought from the recovery room. She was a little nervous, but not afraid, and he felt no worry at all.

"But something went wrong," he told me. "I didn't know what it was, but afterward I found out I'd gone into cardiac arrest. All of a sudden I seemed to be floating. Sounds crazy, doesn't it? I was floating above my own body on the operating table, watching the whole thing and listening. The doctors and nurses were yelling, and the nurses were rushing around. The surgeon was yelling at the anesthesiologist that he'd given me too much anesthesia, and the anesthesiologist was yelling 'The hell I did,' and telling the surgeon he was screwing up the resuscitation.

"I could hear everything, and I was thinking, 'Don't you dumb bastards know what you're doing?' To me, they looked like they were out of control. Here they are, arguing about how come they're losing a patient, and I'm the patient they're losing."

Then he added another interesting bit of information: "I didn't have so much confidence in my wife's judgment after that, either."

"Your wife?" I said. "What did she have to do with it?"

"Well, first, you see, I was floating up there, looking

down on myself and the doctors. But then I floated away. I felt like I needed to see my wife, and I floated right out of the operating room, right down the hallway—and there was my wife on the pay phone, calling my mother. I couldn't believe it. She's found out it isn't going right, and she's in a panic and telling my mother all about it. You think I was having hallucinations, right, Doc?"

"No," I assured him, "I've heard stranger things. I've had other patients tell me about near-death experiences, floating above their own bodies and then coming back. Go on, tell me the rest."

"Well, what happened was they'd told my wife there were complications. They said I was in cardiac arrest and they were trying everything but it didn't look good. So my wife was frantic, and she was babbling all about it to my mother while there I was, floating above her. I could tell my mother wasn't believing it. She was insisting it was just a simple operation and what could go wrong? I don't know what my wife said after that, because the next thing I knew I was floating up higher, up into some kind of tunnel of light. Then there was someone in a white robe, this figure in a white robe. I couldn't tell you what his face looked like, it was just this figure in white, telling me I had to go back, it wasn't my time. Here's something really weird, Doc. I knew it was right, that I had to go back, but I almost regretted it. I mean, going back to life with all the pain and problems. It was really peaceful in that tunnel. I felt so peaceful, I didn't really want to go back."

For Harry, that seemed to be the end of the story—or the end of anything worth telling. He stopped talking and I had to ask him, "What then?"

"What then? The next thing I knew, I was back in bed. It must have been a while later, because I was awake. Very groggy, but awake. My chest burned where they'd put the resuscitation paddles. Then, I guess it was some time later, but the next thing I remember my wife came in, and she bent down and kissed me. 'Honey,' she says, 'I'm so glad you're alive.'"

"Don't 'honey' me," I said. "What do you mean, calling Mom like that? You know how excited she gets, and with her heart. You could've killed her."

"You should've seen the look on my wife's face. There was no way I could've known she called my mother, and she started to deny it, but I told her exactly what she said. I mean, I was *there*, I'd heard it, so she had to admit it. She was crying, and I was damn near laughing. The only funny part of the whole thing was the look on her face. She just couldn't figure it out. It took me a long time before I made up with her. Don't misunderstand me. She's wonderful—greatest wife in the world. She's just not the calmest person. That's what I mean about her judgment. That's why I have this feeling about doctors. You think I'm crazy, right?"

I assured him I did not think he was crazy. I told him, in fact, that other patients had described such near-death experiences to me and I considered them genuine. I suggested that he read Dr. Raymond Moody's book, *Life After Life*, which would help him validate the experience in his own mind and make him feel more comfortable with it.

I then questioned him about his relationship with his wife; after all, she had panicked because he meant so much to her, and with regard to her judgment on that very frightening occasion, I felt he was being rather hard on her.

He seemed to become aware of that himself as he talked about her and their three children. Despite his tendency to criticize her, it was a good marriage, and he had a great deal to live for—a topic we then discussed at some length. When the figure in white had sent him back from the tunnel of light, he had felt dismay at the prospect of returning to life, but now, years later, he was a relatively happy human being, committed to staying alive and not killing himself "legitimately" or "accidentally" with cigarettes.

It may seem strange, but the testimony of many people indicates that it is not uncommon for someone after a near-death experience to resent remaining alive. Such a person has seen the other side and would rather be there, at peace, than continue the often painful process of living. If I sense that a patient is contemplating an escape back into the tunnel, I offer immediate counsel on the possible ramifications of death, the loves ones left abandoned, the joys of life yet to be experienced, the sense of purpose being fulfilled that life offers, the obligation to experience all that the future still holds in store. I do not think God wants us to play God and resign from temporal existence at will. Fortunately, talks of this kind with my patients have almost always gone well.

In Harry's case, there was no difficulty; he was, as I said, committed to living. With his permission, I discussed the hospital incident with his wife, and she confirmed the story of her phone call to his mother—and his inexplicable knowledge of exactly what she had done and said while he was still in the operating room. After that first long session and its unexpected detour from the apparently immediate problem of smoking, his resistance to hypnosis (to therapy in general and to me as a doctor) steadily dissipated. Perhaps because I had trusted him and taken his account of a near-death experience seriously without the slightest inclination to regard it as hallucination, he in turn could begin to trust doctors. Perhaps, too, telling the story after all that time was a kind of emotional catharsis for him. In any event, the smoking therapy gradually achieved success.

NDE is a concept of which more and more people in this country and abroad are becoming aware, and it is at last being considered worthy of serious study. This is thanks in large part to physicians such as Elizabeth Kübler-Ross, Raymond Moody, and Melvin Morse. The implications and the benefits of awareness are most interesting. Millions of people have undergone this experience, and many have believed they were losing their sanity. Many others have been afraid to disclose what they saw and heard lest others believe them mentally unbalanced.

I participated in an hour-long, call-in radio program on this topic, and we had phone calls from people who said they had been living with the memory of a near-death experience for ten or twenty years. They had burdened themselves with the conviction that they had suffered pathological hallucinations, and were indescribably relieved to learn at last that what they had gone through had been an experience shared by countless others—a phenomenon, in short, that can be considered normal. How much emotional turmoil those repressed memories represent; how much turmoil can be alleviated by the awareness that the inexplicable is normal.

14 ✧ NDE—The Reluctant Returner

Some diseases are terminal, whether or not they are regarded as purely physical, and every physician must face the inevitability that the joy of healing—the reward of countless successes—will sooner or later be tragically interrupted by a failure. I count Sam's case as one of those failures, one that I was helpless to prevent. A strictly orthodox diagnosis would have listed the cause as coronary disease, perhaps with a notation that deterioration was aggravated by constant smoking. I would regard that diagnosis as accurate but incomplete. Severe as his nicotine addiction was, it was a symptom, a manifestation of a stronger addiction: the wish to die in Sam's case, to return to death.

He was forty-five years old, married, healthy enough in outward appearance, and cheerful in his manner, at least until he began to reveal his real problem to me. His relationship with his wife was mediocre, but they had a very young daughter, hardly more than a baby, and he loved the child and was happy in his role as a father. Evidently, however, he was not sufficiently happy. He was not overtly suicidal (by the usual clinical criteria), nor did he suffer from chronic depression; or if he did, he hid it very well. Both of Sam's parents had died of heart disease, and he had survived his first heart attack at the age of forty-two, three years before he came to see me. More recently, on the recommendation of his cardiologist, he had undergone a coronary artery bypass. During surgery he had suffered a cardiac arrest but had been quickly resuscitated, and his recuperation had been uneventful, except that he had resumed his lifelong habit of smoking. He thoroughly understood the danger of his habit but seemed not to worry much about it. His efforts to quit had impressed the doctor as not especially sincere, and finally the cardiologist had referred him to me for help in breaking the addiction. Without question, smoking was going to kill him if he did not stop.

He readily admitted to me that before the bypass operation he had been smoking almost two packs of cigarettes a day, and now he was smoking two and a half or three packs a day on the average. As he talked, I realized I was listening to an otherwise intelligent man. From what he told me of his family, his work, his interests, and hobbies, it became clear that before his experience in the operating room, he had truly wanted to live, but since then, his view of life had somehow changed.

At first I had to question him repeatedly, gently but insistently, to learn what lay hidden under his casually expressed hints that life had lost its importance for him. The more he talked, however, the more candid he became, and finally he revealed what had happened.

While in cardiac arrest during the bypass surgery, he

had undergone a near-death experience. Such experiences often leave survivors with a reduced fear of death but a profound thankfulness to be returned to life. Sam's reaction, however, was otherwise. As he told me about it, he leaned forward in his chair as if to emphasize how earnest he was and how urgently he wanted me to believe and understand what had happened to him.

"Hell, Doctor," he said, "I might as well admit I'm here under false pretenses. Maybe after this the doctors and my wife will quit nagging me and leave me alone. Everybody goes on and on about how I'll live longer if I quit and I'll die if I don't. So I'll die. That's fine with me. The sooner the better."

Naturally, I asked him why he was so eager to lose his life.

"Doctor," he said, "you can believe this or not, I don't care, but when my heart stopped on that operating table I got a good look at death—I saw the other side. It's hard to describe, but it was like I floated out of my body, up and out, and I was looking down at myself and the whole scene, the whole operating room. I can tell you everything the doctors and nurses were doing. Everything they were saying. You've probably read about this kind of thing. They say you go up into a tunnel of light. I've read about it and that's how they describe it, I mean people who've had that experience. Well, I'm here to tell you they're right. That's just how it was. Only nobody can really describe it. I can't tell you how peaceful it was, nobody can get that across so you'd understand unless it happened to you. It's a peace like no one can have on this side."

"But you came back," I said.

"Yeah," Sam replied, "but it wasn't that I wanted to. I saw somebody up there, in the tunnel, somebody or something I sort of had to obey."

"Who? Who did you see?"

"I don't know. A figure in a white robe, just a figure, pointing. He pointed and I saw Debbie, my little girl. I understood right away. I was going into this light and I knew if I kept going, Debbie would grow up without me. In a way, it was up to me, my decision, but in a way I had to obey what I saw. I didn't come back just because the doctors saved me. I came back because I made the decision. Now I can't help these feelings of regret, these feelings that I want to be back there again, forever, in that tunnel of light, that I need to be there."

"So now life looks different to you? Now it's not worth trying for?"

"Worse than that. I feel like we're born and raised in a prison and just don't know it. Then one day, chance puts me outside the prison. Why me? I don't know, but it happens; I get a peek outside the prison. What I see is this perfect peace. It's a kind of ecstacy. But I came back. I guess you could say I volunteered to come back, so here I am, but I'm also a little resentful. Only now, all I do is wait. I'm just waiting for the light again. Sure, I feel guilty about leaving Debbie, but I can't help it. So tell me, why should I quit?"

I tried to reason with him. I tried hard. I talked to him about the needs of his family, the many kinds of fulfillment to be found in life, the wonders of watching his child grow up, the crime of the thinly veiled, slow-motion suicide he was committing. But in the end it did no good. The patient left me, determined to return to the light sooner rather than later.

About six months later, Sam got his wish. Now Debbie will have to grow up without her daddy.

15 ✧ Leaving the Body for a Clearer View

The phenomenon known as an out-of-body experience (OBE) is somewhat similar to the near-death experiences described in the previous two chapters, but there are significant differences. The experience may occur with or without the prospect of imminent death, and there is no passing into the tunnel of light, no perceived figures or beings directing the spirit back to the body as in accounts of NDE. Instead, the subject simply visualizes—perceives—himself or herself leaving his or her body and going elsewhere. The out-of-body self may journey only a few feet, hovering briefly behind or above the body, or may travel hundreds or thousands of miles before returning to a normal state. The first question, of course, is whether the phenomenon is real or imagined.

It is easy enough to imagine yourself in a place other

than where you are. For example, just close your eyes and picture yourself lying relaxed on a warm beach. Interestingly, there are a few people who have difficulty doing that, but most of us can easily imagine ourselves being elsewhere. What can distinguish OBEs from mere imaginings is the intensity with which the person believes—positively knows—he or she has left the body.

But this brings up a second, related question: Was the vividly remembered OBE real or could it have been, say, a psychotic state of detachment? A profound sense of detachment can be a symptom of severe mental disturbance. A patient is likely to be understandably reluctant to reveal an out-of-body experience for fear that it will be regarded as a hallucinatory sign of psychotic detachment. For the same reasons, therapists must be wary of these accounts.

Yet, I firmly believe that in some cases OBEs do occur. If one accepts the reality of NDEs, I see no logical reason not to believe in OBEs. In both phenomena the spirit, or some of it, temporarily leaves the body; it is just that the reasons are different. Moreover, clinical findings support the logic of belief. There have been cases in which the person brought back some information that he or she could not otherwise have known. There have also been cases in which physical or physiological changes immediately followed an out-of-body experience.

OBEs may occur with or without apparent cause. Some people report that they wake up in the middle of the night to find themselves floating above their bodies. Some have said that with concentration and practice, they have learned to will themselves into this state. They tend to describe the experience as fascinating but frightening. A major fear is the notion that perhaps they will not be able to get back into their bodies. Another is that, while the spirit is out of the body, another spirit might enter and occupy it.

I count myself very fortunate to have encountered people who have undergone out-of-body experience, for I am still learning and will always be learning about the countless ramifications of the spirit. The first such person I encountered was a young truck driver, Mike, who was brought to the emergency department of my hospital years ago when I was working in emergency medicine.

Mike was in the intensive care unit and in very unstable condition. Four days earlier, he had been driving his car while drunk, had crashed into a tree, and had nearly died. The surgeons had inserted a tube into the right side of his chest to re-expand his collapsed lung. He had an intravenous infusion line in his left arm, another intravenous line through which a catheter fed into his heart to measure the delicate pressures within his heart chambers, and a nasogastric tube attached to a suction bottle and leading through his nose into his stomach to decompress any distention and monitor for bleeding. In addition, a urinary bladder catheter was in place to help measure kidney function and monitor for possible urinary-tract bleeding. He did not think he was going to leave the hospital alive.

Upon his initial evaluation and stabilization in the emergency department, he had been told he was about to be taken to the operating room for exploratory abdominal surgery. He had insisted on phoning his wife before signing the consent form, and the staff had overheard him talking to her.

"Honey, I'm sorry. I'm sorry for all the grief I've been causing you and the kids. I've messed up our lives, and now it's too late. I'm not gonna make it out of here. I just want you to know I'm sorry."

Four days later, he still doubted that he would make it out of there, and so did his doctors. He was not fighting to survive. He reminded me of research I had once done regarding the brain-washing of American prisoners of war during the Korean conflict. The goals of that brain-washing included the removal of the will of the captured soldiers to survive. A physically healthy prisoner might go off and sit in a corner, become more and more listless until finally he curled up in a fetal position and—perhaps within hours—died from no apparent physical cause. Mike seemed to have given up in the same manner, and no intravenous tubes or surgical procedures could restore his will to live.

At the age of thirty-four, he saw no reason to continue his existence, and it seemed as if his accident had given him an excuse—a temptation, in fact—to relinquish life. His problems had started very early. He had been the oldest of six children whose alcoholic father had deserted the family when he was eleven years old. His mother could not care for and support six children. The aunt and uncle to whom he was sent let him know very clearly that they had all the responsibility they wanted with their own children and strongly resented his presence. Their home was squalid and unloving, and at the age of twelve he had run away to begin a life on the streets. By the time he was grown and married, he was an alcoholic. The night of his accident had not been the first time he drove a vehicle while drunk, but it seemed it would be the last.

Human beings seem to have two very strong emotional drives: the need to be loved and the need to be needed. During his childhood and adolescence, Mike had experienced no fulfillment of either need. Now he had a wife and three children who loved and needed him but—like many people who have been emotionally impoverished or abused in youth—he had not fully accepted their love. Perhaps he felt he could not trust it. He had distanced himself from his wife and children, retreated into the haze of alcohol. He had even abused them, both verbally and physically. Having known no kindness as a child, he had great difficulty expressing kindness to others. So, as he lay near death, he must have been thinking that his life had been little more than a painful waste.

Four days after surgery, the doctors felt he should be showing significant improvement. Physiologically, there was no reason not to expect him to recover. Yet, his pulse was weak and rapid, his blood pressure dangerously low, his skin ashen, and his lungs still labored to pump badly needed oxygen into his blood. On the sole basis of trauma, the doctors could not explain his failure to show improvement—nor could they explain his very sudden improvement by the end of that same fourth day.

The change was noticed by the nursing staff very soon after a five minute visit by his brother, George. Within twenty minutes after George's visit, Mike's blood pressure climbed back to near-normal, his pulse slowed and strengthened, his breathing eased, and his skin regained color. About all the attending doctors could say was, "Who knows why or how? Sometimes we get lucky and that's just the way it happens."

If I had never seen Mike again, I could not have explained his miraculously swift turn for the better and his subsequent recovery. But I did see him, years later, and— perhaps because I was now a psychiatrist—he decided to confide to me what had happened that day. He had always viewed himself as worthless—unworthy of love and, therefore, unable or unwilling to accept the love of his wife, his children, or his brothers and sisters. He had been conscious when his brother George came to his bedside that day, and quite suddenly he felt himself to be outside of his body, about six feet outside of himself watching and listening to himself and his brother.

George had clutched at Mike's chest as he pleaded with him in an impassioned voice, "Mike, for God's sake, don't die. You can't die. Sheila and the kids need you. Damn it, Mike, your family needs you. They love you, Mike, and you're not gonna let them down, you hear me?"

Mike told me he had never in his life experienced anything like the emotion he felt as he listened and looked down at his brother and himself. He had never thought his life had any value at all, yet he knew instantly that what his brother was saying was true. His family needed him, truly needed him; he had to live, and somehow he knew that his life would now have purpose.

"It was strange," he told me, "really weird. I never experienced anything like that before, and you're the first person I've ever told. I've never even told Sheila, my wife. I mean, I was actually outside of my body, looking down at it, looking down at my brother, listening to both of us. George was crying. I never saw him cry before. If he'd ever said anything like that before, I wouldn't have listened. Only now I knew it was true. I never talked about it because I figured people would think I was crazy or maybe drunk again. But after that, I knew I had some kind of future."

There is just a little more to Mike's story, and I think it worth telling. After recuperating from the accident, he joined Alcoholics Anonymous and has never taken another drink. He has become a sponsor for other alcoholics. No longer abusive, he has developed into a caring husband and father. He still makes occasional mistakes, as do we all, but not as frequently or seriously as he did before his strange experience. He and his brother George have started their own business and are working hard together to make it a success.

Years have passed since Mike's accident, and he has yet to have another out-of-body experience. Perhaps he never will. I like to think that the single episode of literally stepping aside and taking a good look at himself was what he needed to begin building his life at the age of thirty-four. At last he had acknowledged and accepted love and realized his existence was not purposeless. For Mike, I believe love and purpose were truly a matter of life and death.

16 ✧ Summoning Help from Loved Ones

An editor of my acquaintance told me that one morning, several years ago, he felt an uneasy sensation that his mother needed help. He imagined— "saw"—her lying on a sofa in her living room, sick or injured. When he drove over to her residence, he discovered that she had suffered a heart attack and had been rushed to a hospital. She had, indeed, been stricken as she entered her living room from her bedroom and had managed to phone for an ambulance before collapsing onto the sofa. A paramedical team had saved her life. When the son reached her bedside in the hospital, she told him that she had wanted him there but had not asked the staff to phone him—had not even mentioned him to them—because she felt guilty about disrupting his work.

Such incidents are not uncommon. How did the son know that his mother needed him? How was he able to picture her so accurately lying on her sofa? How did she silently communicate with him—call him, so to speak— fifteen miles from where he was working? Incidents of this kind are often ascribed to telepathy, a mental transference of information or emotion from one person to another across space and through barriers, without speech or any mechanical means of communication. We still know very little about the power of the mind or about the power of the energy emanating in one form or another from the mind. I have no doubt that in many instances, perhaps most, these messages are sent and received telepathically, by means within the usual definition of telepathy (thought transference, a form of extrasensory perception.)

Perhaps there is another explanation: that some portion of a person's spirit energy temporarily leaves the body and travels to the person who receives the message.

I find the following account all the more intriguing because the man who wrote it, a retired high school teacher, does not accept the existence of the soul. When he offered to let me use the account of his experience in this book, he commented that he is, at most, an agnostic still looking for answers and not ready to adhere to any particular system of belief. Thus, he has no explanation whatever for what happened to him and feels he must leave its interpretation to the reader. Here is his account:

* * *

I had been suffering from what proved to be an incipient case of kidney stones for almost two years when, near the end of May 1960, I experienced a severe attack. My wife and I, who were employed as teachers in an American high school in a U.S. military base overseas, were back in the States for the summer. Soon after we had arrived at my parents' home in New Jersey, the malady struck.

My father lay near death from cancer, my mother was greatly distraught, and now I was ill. In an effort to spare my bride of less than two years the stress occasioned by these unfortunate circumstances, I persuaded her to pay an early visit to her mother in the South. It was a decision I soon regretted. Several days after she left, my condition grew worse, and I was admitted to the local hospital to undergo tests. By this time my father was in a coma, my pain was excruciating and relentless, and I was profoundly depressed. Consequently, I felt an overwhelming need for my wife.

I suppose I might have had someone telephone her, but after all, it was I who had persuaded her to leave about a week before. I did not wish to seem weak and vacillating. I fancied myself a stoic. It would be better, I thought, if she decided on her own to return.

I was scheduled for surgery in three days. That evening as I lay awake in the dimly lighted room, I remembered how I had called out to my mother as I lay feverishly ill in the sick bay of a naval vessel fourteen years earlier, when I was eighteen. I remembered how my mother on that same evening dreamed that I called to her and knew that I was ill. Now I made a concentrated effort to reach my wife.

I imagined that I left my body and seemed to rise toward the ceiling, looking down at myself still lying in bed. I felt myself leave the hospital room through the closed window and travel through the air, seeing the changing landscape from New Jersey to the South—as if from a plane.

I came to my mother-in-law's house, descended

into it, and stood at the foot of my wife's bed. I called her name and she opened her eyes.

I said, "Come back to me. I need you."

Two days later, I was astonished to see my wife walk into my room—astonished and deeply gratified. I asked her why she had come and if anyone had called her.

She replied, "You called me. The night before last I awoke and saw you at the foot of my bed. You told me to come back. You said you needed me."

Only then, when she told me of her experience, did I tell her what I had done.

Years later, I confided to my mother this strange episode of my wife's hospital visit. I told her how I was prompted to reach out to my wife based on that incident in the Navy when Mother dreamt that I had called to her.

My mother stopped and corrected me. She said, "No, I didn't just dream that. I tried to tell you at the time but you weren't about to believe me. I told you that I woke up in the night and saw you standing at the foot of my bed. You said, 'Mom, I'm very sick!' That's how I knew to contact you."

Those words—"Mom, I'm very sick!"—were exactly the words I remembered calling out from my bed in the ship's sick bay.

*   *   *

You can, of course, simply call these episodes telepathy (whatever that is) and think no further about the actual experiences as related by those who lived them. But that does not adequately explain how the mother of a young man on a naval vessel saw him at the foot of the bed and heard the exact words he called out. It does not explain how, fourteen years later, the same man *experienced* himself leaving his body and traveling a thousand miles from New Jersey to Louisiana to stand at the bed of his sleeping wife and summon help from a loved one once again, or how his wife saw him there and heard his voice, his exact words. It would seem that this man had not one but two out-of-body experiences, both of which brought loving support when he needed it the most.

17 ✧ Fatherly Advice—
From the Departed

Bill and Cathy have been good friends of ours for many years. We share the same sort of appreciation for many of life's values concerning family and the joys of living, although Bill has always been skeptical about spiritual concepts, especially theories about an afterlife. He's always had a view of life commonly described as "realistic," although he knows now that there can be more than one kind of reality—and that all of us must sometimes wonder what is or is not real.

Whereas Bill is pragmatic, Cathy tends to be meditative; she has had spiritual experiences while meditating and—just as Bill always used to know there is nothing worth investigating beyond physical reality—Cathy has always known there is more to the cosmos than we can see or explain.

Even after Bill underwent an experience that defied all his mechanistic views, he was reluctant (which sometimes means afraid) to accept what he could not explain. I think Cathy helped him begin to achieve acceptance, and I like to think I did, too.

Until 1990, Bill held a high-level managerial position with a Fortune 500 company, but during that time of severe economic recession, he was furloughed. Soon he realized the furlough would be permanent; he had lost his job, and, being unaccustomed to failure, he did not take failure well—or what he perceived as failure. Unable to accept the very idea that he had been dismissed, he had difficulty seeking a new managerial position.

Our social visits and dinner-table talks did not help. During the Vietnam War, he had been a Marine Corps officer, and he had thrived on finding pragmatic solutions to tactical problems. In civilian life, he had savored the same responsibility of command, the same logical approach to business problems. When the conversation turned to spiritual matters, he could not help smirking just a little. "Bob," I remember his saying, "you're a great friend and I'm sure you're a great 'shrink,' but people have enough troubles without your filling their heads with this spirit stuff. Maybe they like to hear about the spirit world from some gypsy lady in a carnival but not from the doctor. You'd better be careful, or they'll think you're the one who should be on the couch."

It was good-natured teasing, and I was not about to argue the point with him on a serious level. There was, after all, no way I could shake the foundations of his beliefs, nor did I wish to. Beneath his gentle mocking, he respected my right to my beliefs, and I respected his. But his were about to be shaken by something more powerful than any arguments I could have mustered.

After being out of work for over a year, Bill was finally contacted by a corporation in need of his managerial skills. But the good news was mixed with bad. He wasn't needed at present in the company's New Jersey offices but at a branch in the Midwest. He had been born and raised at the Jersey Shore, as I was, and I could appreciate his attachment to his home grounds. In his case, it was especially strong. He still owned a beachfront summer cottage where he had spent childhood vacations, and his emotional attachment to it was so intense that he had told Cathy he would sell their home if finances forced a sale, rather than sacrifice the summer cottage.

There were no jobs available where the summer house was located, nor was the school system as good as the schools where he and Cathy and their children lived. But such factors failed to move him; he could not bear the prospect of losing the cottage. Nevertheless, he was going to have to accept the job in the Midwest; to make matters worse, he would have to be there alone for the time being, leaving Cathy and the children in New Jersey until he could be sure the new job was right for him and he was right for it.

As he prepared to leave, he was feeling severe pangs of separation. On the night before his departure, in a marked state of depression, he told his wife that he was going to spend one last night in the cottage, alone. It was the next morning that, unnerved, he called me and told me what had happened.

Bill had decided to sleep in his parents' old bedroom—not for any particular reason but on impulse. His mother had died two years previously and his father twenty years before that. He was not mourning but had recently thought fleetingly about his father and their relationship. He had always admired his father and longed to be closer to him, but the father had been somewhat preoccupied with a very demanding job and had seemed to have little time for his son.

As Bill told me about his night in the cottage, he occasionally sobbed, and his voice revealed intense emotion, a side of him he had never revealed until now. "Bob," he said, "I—I don't know how to tell you this. I hope I'm not going crazy. Cathy says I should just accept it, it's perfectly normal. Normal, she says! Maybe she can accept it. I can't."

I tried to calm him, and when his voice was more controlled, I asked him to tell me exactly what had happened.

"Something very weird," he said. "At least, I think it happened. I tried to tell myself it was a dream. Maybe it was. But it was real. I mean it was as real as this right now, Cathy sitting here, me talking to you. You know I never believed this soul stuff, only now I don't know what I believe. I don't even know what I feel. Bob, my father talked to me last night. I woke up in my parents' bed, and there he was, standing there, looking at me. He looked fine—real—my God, I thought he was alive. Not like some ghost in a movie. Real. Solid. It was pitch dark and I could see him plain as day. Bob, he *talked* to me. Even for you this has to be a new one. Am I going nuts?"

I reassured him—and I think he was very glad to hear it—that such occurrences were certainly not new to me. I had heard about similar experiences; I believed him; and no, he was not losing his mind.

He came to see me to talk some more about the strange experience. The room had been totally dark, black, and he could not understand how he could have seen anything at all. He had tried and tried again to persuade himself that it had been a vivid dream. After his father—the vision, or whatever it was—vanished, he got out of bed to see if any light was coming through the blinds. But there was no light. He stumbled as he groped toward the window.

Again I calmed him and tried to give him a brief lesson about the concept of guiding spirits. I told him that it was perfectly all right to believe his father had talked to him—that indeed he probably had—and I asked him what his father had said.

"I actually heard his voice. He told me, 'Billy, it's time to stop worrying and get on with what you have to do. Cathy loves you, the kids love you, everything will work out. I didn't spend enough time with you, I didn't tell you some of the things you need to understand. But you'll never be alone. Now you have to take a chance; grab the chance. It's going to be all right.' Maybe he said more. I'm not sure. But I can still hear him, and that's what I remember. Then he was gone."

Bill had not gone back to sleep for fear the vision would return. He asked me if I thought it would. I told him I could only guess. I shared with him accounts of similar experiences, stories he would never have believed until now. Then I told him I did not think his father would return again soon.

"You needed him," I said. "You needed his visit, his encouragement, and you got it. I'd love to have a visit from my father. His body died fourteen years ago, but I know he'd be there for me if I needed him. But suppose your father does appear again. There's no reason to be afraid of that; he'll be there to help you. Think of all the things you might want to ask him if he comes again. Then, if he does, you'll welcome the experience. There's nothing to dread."

"Yes," Bill said, "I think I can do that. You know, Bob, I had a very odd feeling when I left the cottage. I can't explain it, but for the first time in my life that little house was just a house, like any other cottage in the neighborhood—just a place where people lived for a while, where other people might live later. I'm beginning to believe it really was my father's ghost I saw, and somehow he gave me more than what he said about taking a chance and counting on Cathy and the kids. It was like being released from some kind of attachment I don't need any more. That cottage no longer has some kind of hold over me. I can truly say I can leave it now without any regrets.

Later that same week, Bill moved alone to the Midwest to begin his new job. After he was settled and was handling the position well, Cathy flew out, and together they went house hunting. They obtained a mortgage approval and were about to buy a home out there and sell their New Jersey home when Bill's boss told him he had earned a promotion and would be needed back in the headquarters offices, close to the Jersey Shore. He and Cathy kept their home, and their security seemed assured. It was as if a higher power had been testing Bill's faith and resolve.

The question remains: what was Bill's vision? Was it his father's spirit? These guiding souls, or whatever you wish to call them, seem to me to be like personal trainers or guides who help us negotiate the obstacle course of our lives. In a brief single lifetime, each of us has to conquer fear, prejudice, greed, separations, isolation, and other adversaries to happiness and peace. Whatever we have not learned by the time we die, we may come back to work on at a future time. But for the present, an angel or guide, trainer or even ghost may help us surmount our obstacles. The spirit may appear when needed and whisper what we need to know.

As children, most of us were told there are no such things as ghosts. Later in life we learn—some of us—that very possibly they do exist. There are, of course, many famous stories of ghosts, such as Abraham Lincoln's repeated appearances in the White House. Lacking definitive proof, we must decide for ourselves what to believe. All of the accounts of ghosts that I have heard or read seem to share a common theme: that the deceased subject died with some mission unresolved, some purpose unfulfilled, or some future task to be completed. It is as if the spirit is duty bound not to depart permanently until its tasks are finished. I have included the subject of ghosts in this book because it comes up from time to time with patients. It is an emotionally charged issue that must be addressed. Sometimes a patient who recounts a ghostly experience may be out of touch with reality. But I have known a number of fairly well-adjusted persons who are quite certain they have encountered ghosts. Many such apparitions may be manifestations of post-traumatic stress disorder (PTSD), which is marked residual emotional distress resulting from a tremendously disturbing event. But other cases are not so easily explained, especially when the observer has no prior knowledge of or emotional connection to the deceased and has no clinical symptoms of emotional dysfunction.

The science of physics tells us that energy is neither created nor destroyed but only changes form. What then becomes of psychic energy, spirit energy, when the body it inhabits ceases its life process? Is this energy the mysterious thing we call the soul, and can it take the form of a spirit? A ghost? Could this be akin to what physicists refer to as plasma, the fourth state of matter (the first three states being "solid, liquid, and gas"), which is part energy, part matter (plasma is defined as a highly ionized gas containing an approximately equal number of positive ions and electrons)? Or perhaps we should simply view these apparitions as manifestations of a fifth state of matter and proceed to research the laws of nature that govern their behavior.

POSTSCRIPT

After some deliberation, Bill and his wife decided not to move back to New Jersey. He was enjoying his new job, and the children were enjoying the prospect of their new surroundings. Perhaps his father's message that everything would work out well and there was no need for concern was becoming manifest.

As Easter of 1995 approached, Bill and his family were feeling very much at home in Oklahoma. Some government officials were coming into town for a meeting with representatives from his company. Bill's boss told him to arrange a meeting place away from their corporate offices where they might have fewer distractions.

Bill contacted the appropriate personnel at the Alfred P. Murrah Federal Building in Oklahoma City and secured approval to hold the meeting there. But then he thought perhaps he might find a quieter location and made an alternative booking.

As Bill, his boss, and the visiting officials were sitting down to meet, they heard a large distant explosion and felt a shaking of their room. It was Wednesday, April 19, and the Alfred P. Murrah Federal Building had just been bombed.

18 ✧ The Old Fireman

Tom is a professional firefighter. His father is also a career fireman, as was Tom's grandfather. Professional firefighters are an interesting group. They are, for the most part, highly trained, physically fit, courageous, tough—hardened by experience as well as training—and extremely loyal to one another. The kind of man who is attracted to such a career is seldom the kind who is quick to seek a psychiatrist, and many firemen, in fact, think you have to be crazy to do that. Fortunately, many metropolitan fire departments have come to regard psychiatric counseling as an intrinsic part of health care, but it was not on orders from his department that Tom first came to see me.

It was because he was struggling, and knew he was struggling, with post-traumatic stress disorder after a terrible fire had taken the lives of six of his comrades. He was experiencing paranoid delusions and severe night-mares. An intelligent and eager patient, he improved with surprising speed under short-term psychotherapy, which included clinical hypnosis. After two months, he was functioning normally, a happy and well-adjusted man again, his therapy complete, and I didn't hear from him again for about two years. Then I received a some-what puzzling phone call.

"How're you doing?" I asked. "Have any problems re-surfaced?"

"Oh no, nothing like that," Tom replied. "It's some-thing else, and this time you're going to think I'm really going crazy. Can I come see you? I don't want to tell you over the phone; it's a long story."

When he arrived at my office, he seemed uncharac-teristically nervous. Something seemed to have shaken him. For a few minutes he talked about everything ex-cept the purpose of his visit. Most people are reluctant to share their innermost feelings and even more reluc-tant to divulge bizarre experiences. They fear that a nor-mal, intelligent person will not believe what they have to tell—which is why I keep, of all things, a crystal ball on my desk. I point to it and say, "Any psychiatrist who keeps a crystal ball around like medical equipment is a shrink you can share *any* story with." They usually smile or laugh, and more often than not the gambit works.

Tom began to tell me his story, and it did indeed have some bizarre aspects. About two months previously, his fire company had been called to a warehouse fire on a dark, cloudy night. The power was out in the building, and they had no layout of the warehouse to help them find their way through it. The smoke was so thick that their lighting equipment was of no use inside the structure.

"Did you ever drive through a thick fog?" Tom asked me. "The headlights shine against a fog that looks like a wall and you can't see past it. It was like that, only much worse. Our lights just didn't help."

A detail of men had gone in, groping through the smoke. Tom and the others working outside lost radio contact with them. In the noise and confusion, Tom followed in after them, alone, looking for his men and dragging a hose line so that they would be able to follow it back out. He found that four men had fallen through a large trap door on the ground floor, and some stored appliances had fallen through the burning floor, landing on them. By that time, Tom's oxygen tank was almost empty, and he went out again as fast as he could to get more manpower and a fresh oxygen tank.

He and a couple of others managed to bring out three of the fallen men, but could not budge the fourth. He was unconscious, pinned under a large freezer. They could not lift the freezer and their oxygen was again almost gone. Moreover, the unconscious firefighter was such a large man that they would not be able to maneuver him up through the trap opening, which was now partially blocked by fallen timbers and boxes. As the officer in charge, Tom made the toughest decision a firefighter has to face. He ordered his men to abandon the fallen firefighter and to get out while they could still leave under their own power. He did not think the injured man could hear him, but he told him they would return and get him out of there.

As quickly as possible, he reported to his battalion chief, who agreed it would be useless to go back in the same way and suggested going in through a hatch that led to the basement. Tom went in again, taking with him the only two men available, a rookie and an older fireman near retirement. The inexperienced young man was obviously fearful as he tried to grope through the blinding smoke, but they were not going to leave a fallen comrade to die. Courage is not the absence of fear but the ability to overcome it.

"Sometimes," Tom told me, "I don't know what to do next in a situation like that—and that's the worst part of it. I'm a pro. I should always know what to do. You know what I'm trying to say?"

All too well, I thought, and I nodded as he continued.

"At times like that, maybe it sounds odd, but I ask my grandfather for help. 'Poppy,' I say, 'what do I do now?' He died when I was nine, but even then I thought he was the greatest fireman who ever lived. So I ask him, and would you believe I always get an answer? It happened again this time. I could hear him say, 'Put out your right hand, Tommy. There's a masonry wall. Follow it. Just follow it as far as it goes.' So I reached out, and there was the wall. I got to the end of it—and here's the really weird part. It was still dark in there and smoky, but as God is my witness I saw Bill there—the guy who was trapped— and he was glowing. About twenty feet away from me! I could even see he'd vomited. He was glowing in some kind of white light, and there was a yellow glow right over his head. I thought, my God, he's dying and his soul is leaving his body! The two guys with me, they didn't see a thing—just me."

Tom guided the others to where Bill lay, and this time they managed to lift the freezer away. But by that time, their oxygen was once again gone. Then Tom heard his grandfather speak again: "It's time to go, Tommy." He could not be sure Bill was alive; and if he was, Tom feared he would die if they left him again. But he heard his grandfather repeat, "Tommy, it's time to go."

He and the two other rescuers found their way out, following a hose they had laid down. Five fresh rescuers then went in the same way and—with the freezer no longer pinning Bill—they were quickly able to get him out. By the time he reached the hospital, he had regained consciousness.

"They tell me he'll probably be as good as new," Tom said.

"That's a wonderful story," I said. "Bill owes his life to you. But I don't understand what's troubling you. You and the others saved his life."

"It's a couple of things, Doc. First of all, what if he'd died? I mean, I left him twice and he could have died."

"What about the other part, I mean about his soul? I saw it. Either I saw it or I'm going crazy. What about hearing Poppy—my grandfather? How do I explain that?"

Sometimes psychiatry and spirituality walk the same path. I believe Tom did indeed see Bill's spirit or soul— whatever you choose to call it—and I told him so. I understood, too, about the advice his grandfather gives him in times of need. I told him that, as well, and eventually persuaded him to accept it as a gift of the most wonderful kind.

I have a similar feeling about my own father and how he helps me in my work. Dad was a marvelous counselor, though not by vocation. When I was a teenager, some of my friends liked to come to my house as much to talk with him as to do things with me. Ever since he passed away in 1979, when I need sound advice, I have only to ask, "What would Dad tell me to do?" I cannot say I _hear_ him in a physical sense, as Tom hears his grandfather, but I see no reason why that must be essential in every case. An appropriate answer never fails to occur to me. Is it my father's spirit communicating with me? Or is it just that I came to know his approach to problems so well that by asking him—by thus detaching myself a bit from such problems—I receive an answer of the kind he would have provided?

I gave Tom some reading matter about near-death experiences and related phenomena. He is no longer in need of therapy. He tells me he considers himself lucky to have found a doctor who keeps a crystal ball.

19 ✧ Useless Tubing

In the early chapters of this book, I described some of my experiences as a medical student and as a young doctor specializing in emergency medicine—experiences that influenced my outlook when I became a psychiatrist. Now I want to relate another such experience, because even though it took place during those years and did not involve psychiatric counseling, I feel the incident qualifies as a case study. It was, after all, a clinical occurrence, and it demonstrates a major concept affecting my practice of psychiatry. This concept, in fact, is an important force in the lives of some of my current patients.

It began at half past seven on a September morning at Martland Hospital in Newark, New Jersey. I had just begun my third year of medical school and was now in my first week of clinical studies, which was in pediatrics. Having transferred to New Jersey Medical College from Guadalajara, Mexico, I was feeling some anxiety about my ability to perform well in this exciting and difficult new environment. The demands of clinical rotations (trainings) include not only medical knowledge but stamina, vigor, determination, and occasionally a kind of creative initiative.

One of the patients assigned to me was a two-month-old African-American baby. She had been severely battered by her mother's boyfriend. Perhaps she had been wet or hungry or suffering from colic or—who knows what—and when she had begun screaming and could not be quieted, the man had become furious. He threw her across the room, and her head struck a wall. Jim, the intern in charge of my instruction for this six-week period, had told me to take daily measurements of the circumference of the infant's head. These measurements would provide a rough indication of intracranial swelling from possible bleeding.

On that morning, however, I discovered I did not have my measuring tape in my bag of instruments. I looked about for something to wrap around the baby's head that later I could measure. I spotted a neonatal (newborn baby) suction catheter, a long, thin piece of clear plastic tubing which, when attached to a suction pump can be used to remove fluid secretions from an infant's nose, mouth, or respiratory tract.

These suction catheters are kept individually wrapped in sterile packets, and they are not inexpensive. At first, I hesitated to waste a catheter to take the measurement, but perhaps because I had much to do and was in a hurry, I decided to go ahead and use it. I removed the tubing from its long, sterile envelope, marked the circumference on it, and then immediately realized that I could have taken the measurement without even opening the sterile bag. I could just as easily have used the long envelope itself, with the tubing still sealed inside it instead of wasting the catheter. I could have taken the measurement and afterward replaced the bag where I had found it on the nurse's cart. But it was too late, and I had more pressing matters to attend to.

After recording the circumference on the patient's chart, I had no further use for the tubing. I was about to toss it into the trash can when something seemed to tell me to hold onto it. I did not know why, but I felt I had to keep it. I stuffed it into my back pocket and went on about my morning duties.

When I finally was able to sit down for lunch, I felt the now-forgotten catheter still in my pocket and thought I had now better throw the thing out before Jim, my intern, could see me walking around with a piece of contaminated equipment sticking out of my back pocket. But as I reached for it, once again something told me to keep it. At least six more times during the course of that day, the thought came to me again that for some unknown reason I needed that catheter—or I would need it before long.

It was after eleven at night before Jim and I had taken care of all our duties. "Let's go down to the E.R.," he said, "and see if anything's happening down there."

In the break room next to the emergency cubicle, Jim and I had a cup of coffee and started to chat with the other students, interns, and residents who were on duty. Suddenly, we heard a commotion, and a woman rushed past the security guard into the break room. She was frantic. In her arms, she clutched a newborn infant who was grunting, struggling to breathe. Jim grabbed the baby and we rushed into the ER cubicle. The child's air passage was obviously obstructed and required immediate intubation—placement of a tube into the trachea—from the mouth to the lungs to let air pass in and out.

As quickly as possible, we positioned the tiny infant's head and neck, but when Jim tried to intubate, a delicate and difficult task with a six-pound child, he found the mouth to be full of mucus and vomitus, and he could not see the small vocal cords between which he had to pass the little tracheal tube. The mouth needed to be suctioned out—and very quickly—before oxygen deprivation could cause brain damage or asphyxiation.

Jim called for a neonatal suction catheter, but there was none. Someone had mistakenly put only adult catheters on the intubation tray, and the ends were too large to fit the infant-size suction apparatus. By then, the baby had ceased breathing and lay motionless.

As the co-workers around me became frantic, I suddenly realized that I had the life-saving length of tubing in my pocket. As I yanked it out and attached it, I had a strange thought: this infant can live because I still have this "useless" object that I've been intending to throw out all day.

I suctioned the baby's mouth, Jim intubated her, and we admitted her to the hospital. The obstruction had been an infectious swelling. Several days later when the swelling had subsided and been healed by medication, she was discharged in the care of her grateful mother. The other baby—the battered infant whose head I had measured with the catheter—also recovered fully. But it was the baby with the clogged airway who remained most vividly in my mind. She had been saved by a useless catheter.

It seems to me that my guardian angel—or that baby's—was on duty that day.

Many years have passed. The intern who intubated the baby was Dr. James Oleske who went on to gain worldwide recognition as the physician who discovered the link between infants with AIDS and their mothers. Dr. Oleske—Jim—and I still occasionally work together as members of the executive board of our alumni association. I think he would agree that some unknown, inexplicable urge—a force beyond my comprehension or his—had guided my actions that day when I stuffed the catheter into my back pocket.

This concept of divine intervention, or a guardian angel, comes up frequently now in my psychiatric work. While some of my patients would laugh at such a notion, others (a surprising number, in fact) believe in it or at least believe in its possibility. For those patients inclined to believe, I have discovered that the concept can be of great benefit in a psychotherapeutic setting.

For such patients, the angel (or divine force of intervention, if you prefer) serves as a guardian, spiritual teacher, and confidante. The angel knows more about the patient than does the patient or the therapist and is always present, with the sole mission of helping the patient learn the lessons needed in life. It is a comforting thought, but does it have a basis in reality?

Because so many patients have confided in me about the concept of angels in their lives, I decided to learn more about the subject. In the course of extensive reading, I have found that many cultures and religions hold to a belief in angels—quite often winged spirits in an otherwise human or partially human form. To the Balinese, they are winged mermaids; to the Vikings, the Valkyries; to the Greeks, the horae; the Hindus speak of the Apsaras; and the Persians of their Fereshta. One version or another of this concept is incorporated into such diverse religions as Buddhism, Taoism, Zoroastrianism, Islam, Judaism, and Christianity.

All the same, an average educated person in Western society understandably has great difficulty in visualizing a large, humanoid, winged supernatural creature—a visualization perhaps evolved from ancient pagan beliefs. To attribute this physical form to the concept is not necessary, however appealing it may be to some indi-viduals and, indeed, to some entire cultures. Consider instead a guiding force.

Perhaps you have had an experience such as driving up to an intersection where the traffic light has just turned green. No other cars are in sight. There is no indi-cation whatever that you need do anything but proceed on your course. Suddenly, for no apparent reason, you slam on your brake. Perhaps your foot just seemed to move to the brake pedal of its own volition, or you had a sense that you must not drive through that intersection, or you heard or think you heard a warning voice. A split second later a car, unseen until this instant, darts across the intersection, its driver ignoring the red light. If you had not stopped, you surely would have been hit.

That kind of experience is accepted by many as a case of angelic or divine intervention. You do not have to see an angel appear in full winged glory to feel its effect.

Nor do you or I have to squelch or hide a belief in this concept for fear of ridicule. George Washington was not embarrassed to speak of an angel at Valley Forge, and others who wrote of angels have included Dante, Milton, Goethe, and the twentieth-century philosopher, Rudolph Steiner. I once gave a talk at a psychoanalytic conference on "working with angels"—my acceptance and use of the concept in my work with those patients who can derive benefit from it. I then polled the audience with regard to any experiences these respected therapists might have had with angelic or divine intervention; a full ninety per-cent responded that they indeed had at least one such experience in their lives. Thus, psychotherapy has gained yet another spiritual dimension—and "Yes, thank you. I'll take help from wherever I can get it."

20 ✦ Healed by an Unknown Persona

This case still puzzles me; and I cannot say what force or forces were at work. It was one of my first cases in the realm of spiritual psychotherapy, or as some might term it scornfully, "Aquarian" psychotherapy.

Martha was a quiet, very pleasant woman in her late fifties. She had grown up in rural Minnesota and remembered many cold, lonely days there during World War II when the men in the area had gone off to war. She had spent some of those years in an orphanage because there was no one at home to take care of her during the day.

Although she had a gently jovial manner, she had sought therapy to relieve what she described as a life-long sense of "lonesomeness." When I inadvertently referred to her feeling as loneliness, she always corrected me and did so in a mild tone of exasperation that was very rare for her.

"Don't you see the difference?" she said. "Not lonely—lonesome."

I tried without much success to comprehend the subtle difference. A grasp of nuances is, after all, part of the art of psychiatry. I think perhaps her feeling was not quite a sense of isolation but of longing for someone or something unknown. She was married, she had a family, and certainly she was not alone, isolated, or without the emotional support of loved ones. Still, she felt lonesome and always had.

She had been in therapy with another psychiatrist, but he had not been able to relieve her melancholy feeling, which did not seem to be depression in the usual clinical sense. He had agreed that perhaps some other therapist might find a key to her problem, and so she came to be in therapy with me for almost a year.

Most of my patients are in short-term therapy, so Martha's case was unusual for me, unusual and disheartening. I could not say that I had made any more progress than her other therapist with whom I consulted; and I was feeling uncertain how to proceed further. Then one afternoon, in the course of telling me more details concerning her family, she unexpectedly mentioned that her sister had had a near-death experience. The sister had described it, and Martha believed it fully. I asked her then if she accepted the existence of the soul and the concept that it leaves the body when we die. She said she did.

At the time, I was counseling another patient who was my first to find a resolution of her problems after going back (under hypnotic regression) and seeing previous lifetimes. It occurred to me that perhaps Martha's problem, too, was rooted in a past life. A further discussion of the soul seemed to be indicated. In talking to her about it, I reasoned that if the soul leaves the body when we die, it seems feasible that it must enter the body at or before birth. If so, where does it come from? This might lead nowhere, but it was worth exploring. Perhaps if we were to go backward in time, we might discover the origin of this lonesomeness that had always been with her.

I had regressed her under hypnosis many times, and she was an excellent subject. The past as she experienced it in hypnosis was extremely real for her, not merely a recollection but a presently felt experience. She always brought a sweater to my office even on hot summer days. She needed to put it on before hypnotic regression because when she went back to her childhood in Minnesota she shivered terribly with a sensation of cold.

I now regressed her to childhood, then back into the womb, and finally—in my words—"back before that." Her facial expression rapidly changed from peaceful to puzzled to astonished. Then she thrust herself forward in her chair, and with her eyes still closed she turned her face toward me and demanded almost fiercely, "What do you want?"

Her tone and expression were so unexpected and intense that I was taken aback. For a dismaying moment I wondered if she might be revealing a multiple personality. But it seemed unlikely that a multiple personality syndrome could have remained hidden or disguised throughout a year of therapy, plus previous therapy with another psychiatrist. All the same, her voice simply did not sound like Martha's as she demanded again, "What do you want?"

I gathered my wits and replied, "I want to help Martha. Will she be all right?"

The persona in my patient's chair—for, indeed, this did not seem to be Martha speaking but an entirely different persona—moved her head from side to side and then said very firmly, "Martha will be all right."

Still uneasy, I asked, "Who are you?"

The answer jolted me: "I am the angel of peace."

I know I must have hesitated, and I probably asked the next question falteringly, but I did manage to ask, "Are there other angels?"

Again she turned her head from side to side, briskly this time, and then said simply, "Yes."

"Who are they?"

"It is enough for you to know that Martha will be all right!"

In my perplexity, I know I must have hesitated again, but if by some miracle I was truly communicating with an angelic entity here in my office, I was determined to find out more, or at least try to. Regaining as much composure as I could, I asked, "Where do you come from?"

The question seemed to irritate her. It was as if my questions were somehow improper. Still with her eyes closed, she thrust her face closer as she replied: "I said it is enough for you to know that Martha will be better."

I decided the time had come to retreat. "Well," I said, "I'm happy that Martha will be well."

I brought the patient back then, out of trance. Once more I was looking at the woman who had sat down in that chair half an hour earlier, and once more her voice was her own. She did not clearly or fully remember the words of the persona, or mine, but was aware in a general, vague way of the encounter under trance. She was as astonished as I had been and was profusely apologetic.

"What was *that*, Dr. Jarmon?" she said.

"Martha, the important thing is how do you feel?"

She thought about it for a brief moment and then replied, "I feel fine, but what *was* that?"

"I have to tell you I'm not sure, but it's not anything to worry about. Let's just see how well you do now."

She made another appointment and, still looking confused, got up to leave.

"What was that?" she said again, shaking her head as she left the office. I phoned her that evening to make sure she was all right. She said she felt strangely different and—more important—the lonesome feeling was gone. It was wonderful she told me, suddenly not to feel lonesome any more.

When she arrived for her appointment the following week, she said she had not told anyone what had transpired, not even her husband. She was still feeling great but also still baffled. "What *was* that?" she repeated. I had no better answer for her than when she had first asked.

We repeated the hypnotic induction and regression, but this time I was better prepared. Aware of her religious beliefs, I held a crucifix in one hand, although I had no idea whether it might help me or be needed in any way in communicating with the patient or with the angelic persona. There was no way to predict even whether the persona would come forward again. I rather expected it to, however, and I was not disappointed. Once more, the transformation took place. Prepared or not, I was still slightly unnerved when the voice demanded, "What do you want now?"

"I just want to be sure Martha will continue to be well. She came to me for help, and I need to be sure I've given it—that she'll be well."

I still remember and must confess that as I said those words, I felt a little foolish. My concern for the patient was genuine, of course, but even as I was speaking, I wondered if my statement sounded as if I were fawning, trying to ingratiate myself with this persona. Perhaps what I had said would further irritate this strange being.

"I told you," she said, "Martha is healed now."

The tone of the voice was firm but didn't sound irritated. Perhaps I was being defensive and merely imagining the irritation. I decided to venture further, in fact, to ask if my efforts at communication had offended her.

"Are you irritated with me?" I asked. "You seem—annoyed."

"You summoned me too quickly."

The voice was intimidating; but it had replied. It had not peremptorily dismissed me, and I began to believe I might be able to initiate a true dialogue.

"May I ask where you come from?"

"Do not ask so many questions. It is enough for you to know that Martha is better."

With that, she leaned forward, closer to me. Martha's eyes were still closed, yet I had the feeling this persona was examining the air—the aura perhaps—around my face.

"What are you looking for? May I help?" I asked.

"I want to see if you have honesty."

"And? What do you find?" I asked with some hesitation.

"There is sufficient."

I realized that further questioning would be futile and might possibly elicit hostility, the last thing I wanted for myself or my patient. It was time to bring Martha out of trance.

"Dr. Jarmon," she said, "that wasn't me. I don't know who or what that was, and I apologize for whatever came out of my mouth, but believe me, that wasn't me."

I did believe her, and I told her so. After I reassured her, she went on:

"I don't know what happened, but I know I'm different now, and that bad feeling I've had all my life—that miserable lonesomeness—it's left me. I know we're finished now. I want to thank you for what you've done for me. I mean, I know it wasn't you who healed me. It was something else. But you were here—like a conduit—to let it happen. I feel wonderful now."

A few months later, Martha called me just to let me know that everything was fine. She had kept one more appointment with the other psychiatrist because it had been scheduled and he wanted to see how she was getting along. Dr. DiFeo had been very pleasantly surprised at the change in her. I asked her what he thought about her experience in my office—about the visitation of the persona, or angel of peace, or whatever it was.

"Oh, I couldn't tell him about that," she said.

"Why not?"

"I wouldn't want my psychiatrist to think I'm crazy, would I?"

Several years have passed. Martha sends me a Christmas card each year. She is still well and happy. We still have our little secret, and I still do not know what happened there in my office.

21 ✧ The Lonely Shepherd Persona

We all know that appearances can be deceiving, but sometimes a patient's physical appearance and demeanor drive the point home with particular force, so strong is the contrast with the realities hidden inside. Eileen was thirty years old, the mother of three children, a very plain-looking, overweight woman whose only physically attractive aspect—or so it would seem—was her red hair. She did not conform to our society's standards of feminine physical beauty, nor was her personality or intellect of the sort that would captivate a young, handsome, well-educated, energetic, and ambitious man. Nonetheless, just such a man would soon be revealed as a central part of her problem. His obsession with her would be a problem for him as well.

She came to my office to seek relief from chronic depression which seemed at first to stem from her lot in life. She had grown up in a blue-collar Irish neighborhood of a large industrial city. Her husband, family, and friends were blue-collar workers with little formal education and few interests outside of their community: sports, playing the lottery, and enjoying an occasional night out. Like her family and friends, she had no aspirations beyond the life she knew and might have been moderately content with her home situation but for one tormenting secret passion.

For seven years, she had been having an illicit affair with a thirty-year old college-educated Jewish stockbroker. She and her lover, Stephen, both knew that their families would disown them if their affair were revealed, and neither of them could have faced those consequences.

Eileen was profoundly, painfully aware of how ill-suited they were for each other. They did not share a single common interest. They did not view life, success, or happiness in the same way. They did not fully understand each other's deepest concerns. Even their manner of speaking was totally different. She described him to me, not with pride or happiness, but with bewilderment.

He was, she declared, tall, very handsome, well-dressed and professional looking, extremely successful in his brokerage business. He had never married, and she said he had told her he could not because of his infatuation with her. Far from pleasing her, this situation seemed to make her all the more miserable. She felt that if only he could let go of her and get on with his life, she could let go of him and get on with hers: only that could make her happy—make them both happy. But it was as if they were chained to each other. Her plight, their plight, seemed hopeless to her.

I listened attentively, trying to communicate understanding and sympathy. But at first I was skeptical of the

facts as she presented them. The more details she added
to her description of him and her account of their mutual infatuation, the more it sounded to me like a bored,
frustrated young matron's fantasy—wishful thinking,
daydreams, the sort of fantasy that might be spawned by
television soap operas or paperback romances. If Stephen
is really so wonderful, I thought, why is he so obsessed
with this rather unappealing woman that he can't seek
someone more attractive, more suitable, more appealing to a man of his background and interests?

That was my first reaction. My second was to chide
myself for being judgmental—after all, in matters of
taste there is no right or wrong. Furthermore, I told myself I must keep an open mind while probing for the reality of this strange situation. I could render no service
to my patient by refusing to believe her story without
weighing further evidence.

I did what I could in terms of counseling and awaited
further developments that might be revealed during her
next visit. I saw her in private session twice but seemed
to be making little or no progress in relieving her deep
depression. At one point, she described Stephen to me
as her "soul mate," but a strange soul mate indeed,
whose love gave her no contentment but only made her
unhappy and fearful of losing what contentment and
happiness she found with her family and wished desperately to keep. Yet, in spite of the misery and fear, she
could not, would not let him go, and I was compelled to
tell her so. This, she said, she knew very well. It was why
she had sought my help. She *wanted* to let him go and
was desperately looking for some way out.

It was the patient, I must confess, and not the psychiatrist who thought of something that might sever or
unlock the chain that held the paramours prisoner.
During her third session with me, she asked if I
thought it might be helpful for me to see Stephen in

therapy. Of course it would! Here, I felt, was a young man who needed help as much as she did. Besides, I needed to see for myself what sort of man he was, whether he really was anything like her descriptions. I did not want to raise her hopes beyond reason or probability, however, so I was careful not to sound overenthusiastic when I replied, "Yes, that might help."

I was not sure he would call for an appointment. Remember, I was not even sure he existed, at least as she described him. But he did call that very evening. When he arrived for his appointment, I was surprised to see that he was all she had said he was: tall, handsome, well-built with dark, curly hair, impeccably dressed, well-spoken, calm, and outwardly self-assured. He exuded confidence and control. He did not seem to be the kind of man who would shackle himself to a woman who displayed little charm. I was becoming even more puzzled.

His story accorded exactly with hers. He felt bound to Eileen, could not fathom why, and wished to be free. Except for his inexplicable fixation on this plain-looking, rather dull, and uncultured mother of three, he seemed almost healthier than normal. In fact, he struck me as a rather intuitive person and also an ambitious, aggressive young man on his way up in the world of business and society. Inquiring about his involvement with her as tactfully as I could, I asked—though not in so many words— what he saw in this woman.

Indeed, he told me he had been struggling with that quandary for seven years. Far from idealizing her, he was blunt, almost resentful in talking about Eileen. "I know," he said, "she's not very bright, and she acts a little neurotic. She's not even good looking. I could do a lot better. I mean, I'm not bragging, I've had plenty of chances. But I just feel as if I have to be around her, almost as if I have to take care of her—that I have some kind of duty, some obligation. We've talked about it, you know. It sounds ridiculous, I guess, but we've told each other it feels like a leftover connection from some other lifetime. We've talked about it again and again. Makes no sense, does it?"

We had four more sessions during which we examined every aspect of the relationship and any detectable, motivating factors, conscious or unconscious. The puzzle remained. I had only recently begun to explore and make use of past-life therapy and still was not sure what to make of it, but if ever there was a case that seemed appropriate for this therapeutic modality, surely this was one. I decided to suggest it.

"I've had some patients," I remarked, "who found a resolution to problems or symptoms when I put them into hypnotic trance and they visualized scenes that appeared to be from another lifetime. I'm not prepared to tell you whether the images they see are real—things that actually happened in previous lives—or figments of their imagination. It doesn't really matter as long as the experience provides insights into problems and helps the patient. What I'm getting at is that I suspect we might find hypnotic regression useful for you. How do you feel about it?"

"Why not?" he said. "I'll try anything that might end this thing. I've really got to get free. Hell, so does Eileen."

Although he had never previously been hypnotized, he accepted the procedure easily and soon went into deep trance. I then directed him to travel back in time and place to where he was previously connected somehow to Eileen—or Eileen's soul—to the unknown situation that had been carried over into his present life.

Within just a few moments, his facial expression began to change. It went from peaceful to anguished, and then, quite abruptly, he began to weep. There in my office this man, whose composure had seemed so unbreakable, was suddenly and uncontrollably sobbing. As he cried, he was talking to an imagined young woman, an invisible girl he was cradling in his arms. I could tell that much, but I could not understand his words; he was speaking a foreign language.

I was able, gently, to break in on the scene he was visualizing, and I began to question him. To my relief, he replied in English, and his story began to unfold. He was, he told me, an eighteen-year old shepherd living near the Mediterranean coast. He was in love with a young woman of his village, and they had planned their marriage with the blessing of both families. But she had become ill and began to waste away; it sounded to me as if perhaps she was suffering from cancer. Then, she was dying in his arms as he begged her not to leave him. She was apologizing to him! She was telling him how sorry she was for the pain her death would bring him. He cried as all of this came back to him. With heart-wrenching sobs, he promised to be with her again.

Just as I had been initially skeptical when Eileen told me about Stephen, now I felt myself wondering whether I was hearing fact or neurotic fantasy. But I could see no way that doubt—most especially expressed doubt—could help my trusting patient who was counting on me to heal his psychic wounds. I owed it to him to return his trust, or try to, and to counsel him in a manner that would release him from a bondage of mourning that—regardless of whether it was real in a physical sense—was tormentingly real in its effects on his current life and that of Eileen, my other deeply distressed patient.

I guided him forward through the previous incarnation he was describing, and he told me that he had lived into old age—lived a dull and sorrowful lifetime, never marrying, mourning for the woman he would have married. I felt I understood now; the melancholy mystery was unlocked, and it was time to bring him forward into his present life and to help him free himself.

"Now," I told him, "her body from that past life is dead. You could never have prevented her death, and you honored your commitment to her longer than was needed. Her soul long ago went on to the resting place and has come back now in another body. But she's a different person, her life is different now, and it can be a contented life. It wasn't your fault that she died. Eventually, you died, too, and came back. You kept your promise, you met her again, and that frees you both. You're free of those obligations formed in an earlier lifetime. It's time for you to go your separate ways. She has her mate, she'll have contentment without you, and you need to find your new mate in the present, in your current life."

As I heard myself intoning those words, I also heard a small voice inside my head ridiculing me, telling me I sounded like a mystical guru and asking with deep sarcasm where in my medical training I had absorbed such concepts. In those years, I was still unsure of my ground, still fearful or skeptical of the implications inherent in such counseling.

I brought Stephen out of trance and asked him how he felt. For a few moments, he was slightly groggy but soon became alert and intensely interested in what had just transpired. I asked him if he was aware of what he had talked about.

"Yes," he said. "Well—vaguely."

I told him in detail what he had said. "What now?" he asked. "What does it mean? I can see what it says about Eileen and me, but is it real? I don't know if I can accept it. What do you think, Doctor, will we be free now?"

"I can't answer you for certain," I admitted. "If it resolves your dilemma, you're cured. If not, we have more work to do." (Well, I thought to myself, that was spoken like a true psychotherapist—avoid flat statements at all costs, just in case.)

Before leaving the office, he made an appointment to

see me again the following Thursday, as usual. But two days later, he phoned to cancel the appointment. He was about to leave town briefly. He had run into an old girl-friend; they had immediately felt a strong mutual attraction, and they were off for a week of skiing in New England. She was bright, beautiful, and fascinating—the antithesis, he told me, of Eileen. Perhaps his comparison was callous, but if so, it indicated that the shackles had been broken.

"What about Eileen?" I asked.

"She's fine," he said. "Doesn't even want to see me. I'm not sure what happened in your office, Doctor—maybe I'll never know—but it's very strange. I don't feel any attachment to her at all. Nothing, ancient history. So whatever you did, thanks. Eileen thanks you, too. I'll certainly know to call you if I ever need help again."

That was several years ago. I have not heard from either of them since.

22 ✧ Terror Under a Full Moon

George was a well-dressed, well-mannered, well-spoken forty-two-year-old businessman, highly regarded in his community even though—as I eventually discovered—the police had once been called to his home to quiet a domestic disturbance. His wife, Maria, brought him into my office in the hope that I could do something about "George's period"—a term they both used to describe what had been happening once a month for more than twenty years. At the time of the full moon, George became inexplicably agitated. Sometimes, in fact, this calm, friendly gentleman became a frightened, hostile mass of irrational energy. At such times, he seemed to feel that, wherever he was, he was in danger and must flee. Often he was on the brink of leaving his wife and home, running away. When asked where he would go, he had no idea and did not care. He just felt the compulsion to escape.

His symptoms had first begun to appear at about the age of twenty. At that time, he also spontaneously developed a seizure disorder, to which his monthly bouts of paranoia might or might not be related. CAT scans and electroencephalograms had revealed only an area of scarring in the left temporal region of his brain, the cause for which was never determined. The seizures had been controlled with Tegretol and phenobarbital, and the patient was still taking the latter medication when he came to see me. The periodic paranoid behavior had never been addressed.

Maria persuaded him to seek my help because his intense emotional episodes were taking a severe toll on her own emotional health. During several of his recent "periods," he had been ready to abandon everything: his wife, his home, his career. He just "had to get away— fast," as he told me, and added that he felt he would die if he did not flee.

He and Maria had been married about two years when she realized that his paranoid behavior always occurred at the time of the full moon. When I was a senior student at New Jersey Medical College, I wrote a research paper on the statistical relationship between certain environmental and atmospheric factors and crimes of passion in the City of Newark. One of the factors with a high degree of correlation to certain crimes was the full phase of the moon,[1] a phenomenon familiar to the police. I did not have the opportunity to explore the possible causative influences, and after my research was presented and published, I pursued the subject no further, as I had to get on with the rest of my medical training. I never expected that decades later I would be addressing the subject again.

During his first office visit, George was the picture of

composure—affable, a fluent conversationalist, a man with a ready smile. Many people, including psychotics, can make a good impression even while disturbed. But the accounts of his behavior during the full moon were hard to fathom.

We proceeded with a standard psychiatric interview, and nothing emerged that might account for the bizarre behavior described. Our second and third sessions went much the same way. But our fourth session was scheduled to coincide with the full moon, and I hoped I might then gain a better sense of what I was dealing with. I was not disappointed.

George and Maria arrived in separate cars. He was markedly agitated. He could hardly sit in his chair. His eyes darted about the room as if he were expecting that at any moment he would be caught by an unseen enemy.

He said, in a somewhat aggressive tone, that he had insisted on driving his car to my office because he intended to leave Maria as soon as the session was over. When I asked him precisely what he intended to do, he said he would just get into his car and leave as fast as he could. He intended to abandon his job, possessions, everything. Fear and bewilderment clearly showed through the bravado. He could offer no explanation save that he just had to get away.

I was able to persuade him to do some deep breathing and guided imagery exercises, calming him down and taking him into a relaxed state, but it took some time. That was as far as I got. I had not yet begun hypnosis when my next patient arrived. I had to end the session, but at least I had glimpsed the behavior that had brought him there.

Evidently, his state of tormented agitation soon subsided, for he did not leave his wife and he showed up the following week for another scheduled session. Having felt somewhat uneasy about ending the previous session without rendering much help, I was relieved to see him. The full moon was now waning and so were his apprehensions. Early during his fifth visit, I took him into a hypnotic state. He proved to be an excellent subject, going into trance deeply. Perhaps now some progress could be made.

I directed him to go back in time to when his anxiety about the full moon started. He unhesitatingly related how as a teenager, while he was working at a summer job on a moonlit night, three friends had stopped by and invited him to join them. He could not get off duty. The friends went on without him. They died that night in a freak automobile accident.

He told the story with little display of emotion, but I thought perhaps we had found the root of his anxieties. I gave him the sort of healing affirmation previously described in this book, assuring him that the death of his friends was not his fault, that he himself had been very fortunate that night, and that he no longer had any cause to feel anxiety on nights of the full moon. He did not respond at all as I expected. Instead, he spontaneously seemed to slip into a deeper trance. Now he became emotional, fearful.

He spoke in broken sentences about soldiers, enemy lines, bombings. I did not get a clear picture of what he was relating, but I felt that whatever it was, he had experienced enough for the time being. Again, I gave him a healing affirmation followed by a post-hypnotic suggestion that the next time he went back to that scene he would see it clearly.

Upon emerging from trance, he remembered little of what he had said, so I described what he had revealed about the memory of the night when his friends were killed in the auto accident. It was no surprise to him; he had always consciously remembered the tragedy. But he did not remember anything related to the other experience he had visualized. When I asked him about his vision of soldiers in wartime, he had no explanation.

His wife then told me something she felt might have a bearing on this image of war. Once, when George was suffering through his full-moon paranoia, he became so uncontrollable that she called the police. When they arrived, George ran into the bathroom and cowered under the sink. Judging by what he said, he must have thought the two uniformed men were German soldiers and, speaking German (a language he does not know), he begged them not to shoot him. The police later remarked to Maria that this was not the first time someone had reacted to their arrival in such a strange manner. Perhaps they were merely trying to comfort her, or perhaps such occurrences are not uncommon. In any event, no one knew what to make of it. George's next office visit proved to be the most startling of all. I put him into trance and he went in, as psychiatrists phrase it, rapidly and deeply. He immediately became visibly apprehensive.

"They're going to get me tonight," he exclaimed in a hoarse whisper. "I know it. They'll spot me! I told command we couldn't go ahead with the mission on a night like this. Look at that moon. My God, you could read a newspaper in this light. They'd have to be blind not to get me."

"Who's going to get you?" I asked.

"The Germans. They'll spot us, for God's sake. I told command it couldn't be done—not to make me do it tonight; but they wouldn't listen, they said it had to be done. I believed all that talk about going home. FDR said we'd be home for Christmas, didn't he? It's almost Thanksgiving, and it looks like I'll never see home."

"Where's home?" I asked.

He gave me the name that could be that of a town and said it was in Missouri.

I had no way to be sure what was going on, fantasy or reality, but I had a strong feeling that this was the path my patient needed to take. I asked him about other details of his life: what his name was, where and when he had gone to school, who the members of his family were. He answered all my questions without hesitation.

Then, slipping back into the war scene, he said he was an American officer, assigned to operate clandestinely behind enemy lines during World War II, to help refugees sneak through German lines to the West. The rest of the story was brief and came quickly.

One night, in a small German town under the bright light of the full moon, he was spotted by a German sentry. The exchange of a few words was sufficient for the sentry to realize he was a foreigner. The sentry shouted for help and more German soldiers raced forward. They had no intention of bringing him back to their commanding officer. They knew he was a spy or saboteur, and that was all they wanted to know. They forced him down to a river bank. The light of the full moon was shining off the water and into his face when they shot him in the back and in the left side of his head.

"I'm shot," he said. "My back. My head." Then he was silent.

"And now?" I asked. "Is there more? What happens now?"

"I'm floating into a tunnel of light. There's Joe. Joe went through basic training with me. Haven't seen him since. I guess Joe didn't make it either."

Then he said he saw his mother and father who had died when he was young. After that, he was silent again. It was time to provide the patient with a healing affirmation, though one that was perhaps out of the ordinary. I assured him he had been right to fear the full moon on that terrible night of war. Its brightness did give his position away and he was caught, killed; but the war was over now, long over; he was back in America, and his soul now occupied a new body. He no longer had cause to be terrified of the full moon.

When I brought him out of trance, he looked weary but said he felt strangely light and peaceful. He was not aware of the vast majority of what he had said, so I told him the story in full, as he had told it to me. He was understandably puzzled but not in an unpleasant way. Again he remarked that he felt light, peaceful, and added only that he needed to think about all this.

After that session, he reported that his symptoms of paranoia during the full moon had almost disappeared entirely. The inexplicable sense of foreboding was nearly gone. We conducted two more such sessions, and his symptoms disappeared completely.

Out of curiosity, his wife told me that she looked for and found that small town in Missouri in an Atlas and contacted the high school there. She told the school secretary she was trying to trace the whereabouts of a relative. The secretary looked in the school records for the name the soldier had used and said, "Yes, he graduated here—a year earlier than you said, but that must be him, all right."

I ordered two subsequent electroencephalograms for my patient. They showed no scarring—the scarring had disappeared—and no seizure-like activity (sometimes EEGs spontaneously revert to normal).

A most curious thing took place during the second of these tests, which was a Holter, a portable, twenty-four-hour EEG. I had wanted a Holter EEG so that I could record his brain-wave patterns during hypnosis as he reexperienced his past life as a soldier, his death at the hands of enemy soldiers, and his experience going into the "tunnel of light."

I asked a colleague of mine to analyze the EEG tracings. He is an examiner for the National Board of Neurology and Psychiatry, testing neurologists and psychiatrists on their ability to interpret EEGs. He told me that the brain wave pattern generated when the patient was going into the "tunnel of light" was that of a person in deep sleep, not hypnosis. But my patient was not asleep—he was talking, as demonstrated on the videotape that I made of the session. I asked the neurologist if this could be the pattern of a person talking in his sleep, and he said, "No."

Clearly, more research needs to be done in this area of near-death experiences incorporating the use of EEGs.

That night, while still wired to the EEG recorder, George lay down on his living room sofa to take a nap. He was awakened suddenly by his dog madly barking at someone standing at the end of the sofa. It was not Maria; she had gone up to bed. George looked up and saw to his amazement his old girl friend, Inga, from Missouri, from his previous life. Dumbfounded, he stammered, "What are you doing here?"

There was no reply. She gazed at him for a moment and then faded away, and the dog stopped barking.

That all happened more than four years ago. After struggling with his monthly psychotic episodes for more than two decades, George remained symptom-free. Gradually, he ended his use of anti-seizure medication and had no further seizures as of my last follow-up with him two years later, at which time he moved out of New Jersey.

George had told me that although the experience of seeing Inga was incredibly real, he tried at first to tell himself it was merely the result of awakening suddenly from a vivid dream. But then he realized that the vision had not appeared to him alone. After all, he only woke up because his dog was barking at the stranger in the room.

23 ✧ The Woman Who Hated Money

(When Past-Life Therapy Is Not in Order)

It is our nature to try to avoid unnecessary pain. That is axiomatic. In fact, to seek out pain may be indicative of an emotional pathology. The well-integrated person only chooses pain in order to achieve a greater good such as studying late at night in order to do well on an examination, fighting hunger pains in order to lose unhealthy fat, or straining at physical exercise in order to build up endurance and strength.

So it is that patients strive to avoid unnecessary emotional pain when it comes to psychotherapy. As people have come to hear of my work in past-life therapy, they look to see this as a relatively painless way to put to rest their emotional problems.

I advise patients that when the problems originate in this current life, it is this life's problems that need to be faced. Attempts to side step the pain usually end in frustration.

Such was the case with a woman I will call Alice. She presented an intriguing enigma: a professionally able and successful woman whose business was in constant danger of failure because she could not bring herself to accept its rewards. Why should payment—equitable remuneration for honorable service—be degrading, shameful? She could find no answer.

Alice owned and ran a business providing social work and employee benefit consultation. She clearly knew that her service was skillful, caring, beneficial, and fully appreciated by her clients; yet, she felt extremely uncomfortable, almost humiliated, whenever the time came to accept fair payment for her work.

Many people in the care-giving professions have occasional qualms about this, but Alice's aversion went far beyond that. It had always been a problem for her, but since she was seeing a therapist, she kept holding onto a hope that the aversion would eventually dissipate. The last straw came, bringing her to tears one evening when she realized that, without thinking, she had thrown a large payment check into the wastebasket. She could not afford to throw away her livelihood.

Alice had heard about my work in past-life therapy and hoped that this therapeutic modality might unlock a hidden cause of her problem and heal it. When her story unfolded, however, she and I both discovered that in this case the causative trauma lay buried in the early years of her present life and not in a past incarnation.

As I started taking the patient's emotional history and life review, she recounted a brutalized childhood. Her mother had died three years ago, and with that loss there began to flow a flood of emotions and memories from her early years. But by clouding over many other memories of those years, her mind had erected a defense against intense pain. She had always known that her formative years were spent in poverty and that several of her six siblings were struggling with their own emotional problems, but until three years ago, she had been unable to summon essentially any detailed childhood memories. Whole years were totally shrouded, lost to her conscious awareness.

What had begun to emerge three years ago was a horrific litany of emotional, physical, and sexual abuse perpetrated by her father who had died just as Alice was reaching puberty. She suffered from an intense aversion to accepting money and failed on her own to find a reason for this.

She proved to be a good subject, and with use of standard hypnotic induction, I directed her to go back to where her problem about money originated. The following is a transcription of that session, lightly edited for clarity and confidentiality.

"Let's go back now to where the problem started," I said. "What's happening now?"

(No immediate response. The patient begins to weep.)

"It's all right," I said. "It's okay to cry. You can let it out."

"I'm inside." (Patient continues to weep.)

"Inside? Inside a house, a building? Is it cold? Hot?"

"It's warm." (Patient sobs.) "I'm alone, all alone ... "

"Now go to the next thing that happens. Can you see what you're wearing? Can you feel what you're wearing?"

"I'm little—I'm so little ... " (More sobbing.)

"Now what happens? Tell me the next thing that happens."

(No immediate response; more sobbing.)

"Now what happens? It's okay. It can't hurt you now. What do you see?"

(Long pause before the response.)

"She leaves ... "

"What do you mean, 'She leaves'? Did she leave her

body? Did her soul leave her body? Was that not a good place to be?"

"She left her body."

"Why?" (Pause.) "Did she come to that body by mistake?"

"She doesn't want to be there . . . She didn't want to be born."

"Why? Why didn't she want to be born? Didn't she decide to come into that life?"

"They didn't want her." (Patient sobs again.)

"Did they try to abort her?"

(No response. Patient sobs and clutches at her right shoulder.)

"Now what happens?"

(Long pause.) "I have to come back again."

"Why? Why do you have to come back?"

"Everybody says I should *know* why. But I don't know why."

"It's okay. You'll remember, and then you'll be able to feel better about it. You'll be more at peace."

"I need to love people. I need to . . . "

"Go on. You're doing very well."

"I need to take care of Bill." (Bill, the patient's husband, had died after a lingering illness.)

"Tell me about the problem with money. Why is that? Why have you had trouble accepting it? Another scene is going to start to appear to you."

"It's . . . my mom's living room . . . and . . . he's there!"

"Your father?"

"Yes."

"What's going on now?"

(Patient resumes sobbing.)

"About how old are you now?"

(Patient responds in a childlike voice.) "Five. I'm five years old."

"Is anybody else in the room? . . . Now what happens?"

"He gives them something. He doesn't give me any—he doesn't give me any. I'm bad." (Patient says loudly.) "I'm bad. I'm not good, I'm bad, I'm bad!" (Profuse sobbing.) "I'm bad . . . He never gives me anything because I'm bad, I tell. I tell!" (More sobbing.)

"You tell the truth. Does your father get mad when you speak the truth? Who tells you you're a bad girl?"

"He does. He yells at me."

"And then what happens?"

"My soul leaves my body . . . I have to. I can't stand the pain . . . I'm bad, too . . . He couldn't buy me. He *couldn't* buy me. I'm strong . . . I'm strong . . . "

"You'll never let anybody buy you, will you?"

"No! Never . . . Never . . . Never! Never!"

"When you see money coming at you . . . "

"I don't *want* it! Get it away from me. Get it away . . . Get it away! I don't deserve it. I'm bad. I'm bad. I'm bad." (Patient again sobs profusely.)

"Time went on," I told her, comforting her. "Time passed. Every day that went by, you became a day older. Every year that went by, you became a year older. One day he died, and he was never in that house to trouble you again. God has him now. Now he's the one who must look at all of the horrible things he did."

"I don't want him to hurt," Alice replied.

"He has to learn. We're all here to learn. He now knows the hurt, the pain he caused you. I want *you* to see that he made money have a certain significance for you, a wrong, very wrong meaning. There are many people out there who know you're a good person, and they want to give you money for your good services—and you'll accept that, because you *are* a good person. They have no ulterior motives; they aren't trying to bribe you, to buy your silence. They just know that fair is fair, and they give you money in an entirely different way than your father used to. They give you money because they're grateful for the help you give them, not to buy them off."

As I spoke, I was gratified to see a peaceful expression return to Alice's face. Her body, which had occasionally become tense—rigid—while re-experiencing her childhood defiance of her father's bribery, had again become totally relaxed. It was clear now that he had bribed and threatened her brothers to keep them silent about his abuse. But he had failed to silence Alice—she had, indeed, been strong. After his death, for so many years after, she had blotted out the memories of the abuse, the threats and attempted bribery, and the aftermath of additional pain when she refused the bribes and spoke the truth.

I continued my healing affirmation and strongly sensed that my words were having the desired effect on my patient.

"Alice, money now is a validation that you're a good and useful person. That's what money means now—that you have a worth, a great worth. You're a worthy creature of God. Even the worst of us has to go back to God, as your father has. When people give you money, that's just one way they're telling you they're grateful that God put you on this earth to help them, to provide good honest services for them. It's a validation. Be grateful that you have the ability to help people and to earn money. There's nothing wrong with that; it's good. Now you'll see yourself doing a good job, doing it diligently, enjoying the fruits of your labor."

Watching her closely, I could discern something beyond relaxation in her expression. It was a look of peace, contentment. Something about the lines of her mouth, her closed eyes, seemed to indicate a kind of satisfaction akin to pride. I knew our session was close to its successful conclusion as I continued.

"The worst parts of your life are over, long over. Your father can never harm you again. He regrets what he did, regrets it deeply. He knows he's going to have to come back and pay for that, and he will. But he knows, too, that you don't want to hurt him, you'd never hurt him, and you won't, ever. Now just rest, and heal in the light. Be at peace. Soon it will be time to fully resume your life, feeling wonderful about yourself and the good work you do."

There it was—there was the expression on her face that I had been working toward and that she, too, had been working toward: a gentle smile. I brought her out of hypnosis.

The patient was surprised to realize that her money problem had stemmed from her father's abuse. She had thought she had already successfully dealt with the traumatizing events of his mistreatment.

Often, patients arrive with some concept of the causes underlying a problem, and the concept may be correct, partially correct, or incorrect. As a therapist, I endeavor to keep all the fields of possibilities open so that the true origins of ongoing pain or disturbance will not be bypassed or disguised. In this case, Alice discovered that her symptoms were produced by trauma in the childhood of her present lifetime—more than enough trauma to account for a neurosis without any echoes emanating from a previous incarnation. She felt no compulsion to explore the possibility of past lives merely out of curiosity. She was happy to be healing and aware that just a little more therapy would probably be needed in order to definitively put her painful childhood behind her.

PART III

THE ONGOING SEARCH

24 ✧ The Lesson of a Loser

A psychiatrist who says "I have learned all I need to learn; I know my field of study thoroughly" is, I believe, a psychiatrist who has not *learned to learn* and may unwittingly encounter failure at least as often as success. Fortunately for the countless people who need the healer's gentle help, most psychiatrists of my acquaintance have the open-minded attitude of the searcher, the explorer, the perpetual student. Having been privileged to learn much about various therapeutic modalities, I know that I have much to learn still and will go on learning, seeking to learn, for the rest of my life.

Discoveries are made along the way; so are mistakes, and we learn from those, as well. In addition, we frequently gain insights (or *can* gain them) from practitioners of disciplines other than our own. "If the mind were simple enough that we could understand it, we would be so simple that we couldn't." That eloquent reminder was penned not by a psychiatrist but by Emerson Pugh, a teacher and author in the realm of technology, industry, and "hard" science.

In the final section of this book, I will discuss my own ongoing search, past, present, and future, including mistakes, discoveries, and hypotheses for further consideration and investigation. I will begin here with an account of an experience I had with a patient long ago, a patient I was able to help somewhat but not to heal. There is no deep satisfaction in recalling such an experience, but it furnished a lesson that merits presentation. Most significantly, perhaps, it helped me to face a paradox of psychotherapy: that total healing is the essential, constant, but not always attainable goal. There are patients whose time to heal has not yet come.

As a therapist, my life's work is to help people to heal, yet I am coming to believe in a destiny that shapes some lives with a force beyond our understanding or power. Many people would call it karma, specifying the definition of karma as the principle of causality, the consequences of one's actions fixing one's lot in a future existence. In spite of all our efforts, I believe there are some among us whom we cannot save from pain— souls who must endure an unhappy karma, suffering on this plane of existence we call life. However, this belief should not preclude the therapist's endeavors or lead to a defeatist attitude. Every patient is worth *trying* to help.

I believe Frankie was a patient destined to suffer, tethered to a relentless karma. Sadly, he was the kind of person often callously described as a "born loser." Overweight, balding, homely, and bitter, he had grown up in a poor, tough, blue-collar neighborhood in New York. At the age of thirty-seven, he had achieved nothing worthwhile, and although he had frequent get-rich-quick fantasies, he had no real ambition of any kind. His mother used to tell him that when he was an infant he would habitually lie flat in his crib, doing nothing, hardly moving, and he had not changed much as he grew older. His brother and sister had somehow found an ideal that had escaped Frankie—a work ethic.

Some people seem to prosper even without diligence and honesty, but Frankie was not one of them. He was very intelligent, and he seemed to possess an evil streak that inspired disreputable schemes, but he was too lazy to attempt to carry out these plots. One day in my office, as he was raging against his lot in life—typically blaming every possible scapegoat from banks to politicians—he exclaimed, "That's it, damn it. I'm going to blow up the [expletive deleted] Republican headquarters!"

"How are you going to get there, Frankie?" I asked.

He paused, looked at me with puzzlement and frustration, and shrugged. "Oh, the hell with it," he answered. "The bus probably doesn't go there."

Occasionally, he almost seemed to be mocking himself. One day he burst into my office in an excited state and told me: "Last night I finally figured it out, Doc. I finally realized what's wrong with me. I'm a schizophrenic; I've got two personalities." Then, he suddenly looked crestfallen, and almost in the next breath he softly remarked, "No, that's crap, Frankie, we've got it all wrong. That's not it at all." Another time, agitated and frustrated over his inability to accomplish anything, he shouted, "You probably think I'm not doing a [expletive deleted] thing! I'll have you know I'm burning a hell of a lot of energy just spinning my wheels!"

I believe he enjoyed his sessions with me because they struck him as getting something for nothing—a free ride, so to speak. To avoid paying or working for anything had become almost a vocation for Frankie. Seventeen years before I saw him, when he was only twenty, he had been in an accident, hit by a truck. He showed no physical effects, and his injuries probably were minor, but with the help of a clever attorney, he had parlayed the accident into financial security, an insurance settlement that would pay for a certain amount of therapy and would support him sufficiently so that he would never have to work again. For whatever reason, he had been deemed emotionally traumatized and unemployable. Of course, the object of his psychotherapy was to get him "back to normal" under the terms of the settlement, a nebulous concept in Frankie's case. If and when the insurer concluded that psychotherapy could not accomplish that, payments for counseling would cease, though other medical expenses would be paid until the day he died.

I tried most every therapeutic modality, and his case became a kind of ultimate challenge to me, but we were making little progress. He seemed to take a perverse pleasure in his own failures. Far from seeking work, he remarked more than once that he actually avoided employment, because if he ever got a job, he ran the risk of being fired. He concluded that he was much better off remaining "sick." Once, in fact, he admitted that his worst fear was to be re-evaluated and deemed cured.

Although he held tenaciously to that style of existence, Frankie was one of the most unhappy human beings I have ever met. I saw him as the quintessential example of the adage "Be careful of what you wish for—you might get it!" Frankie had wished to never have to work in life. He had gotten his wish and was one of the most miserable people I have ever known. Although he often told me in fits of rage that his hatred and bitterness were bottomless, there was also a tender, compassionate corner of his being. He had wept at the sight of a poor old man, driven to do menial labor for a few dollars a week. Perhaps it was his refusal to exert any effort that kept him from being a destructive sociopath, but I think it was his gentle side.

From time to time he remarked, "I must have been some God-awful son-of-a-bitch in my last life to get all this crap dumped on me in this one!" I was not yet experienced in past-life therapy; but nothing else was working for him, and so one day, almost without thinking, I said half-jokingly, "Well, you're a good hypnotic subject. Why don't we go back and see what you did the last time around to deserve such a lot in this life?"

He very quickly went into a deep trance, and I was soon to regret, or at least question, my decision. A horrifying transformation started to take place within the man seated in front of me. A deep hideous laugh roared out of him like human thunder. His face turned red, as the blood vessels in his skin dilated and pounded. A snarl came over his face, and saliva dripped from his gaping mouth. The entire fifteen-room building seemed to resound with the energy he emitted.

I told myself this could well be the precipitation or onset of a psychotic breakdown, and it would be prudent to return the patient to his pre-hypnotic state as expeditiously as possible. If Frankie were correct in that he was some reincarnated mega-SOB, I certainly would not want to have that persona in my office with me! Heeding the old axiom that discretion is the better part of valor, I brought him out of trance.

That alarming experience was my first real brush with past-life, or reincarnation, therapy. It is a wonder that I ever attempted it with another patient. I marvel at the true nature of evil. Some of my colleagues have interpreted this case as an example of evil possession. With Frankie, I never ventured in that direction again, although he did say he felt better—"somehow lighter"— after that session. A voice inside me seemed to be warning, "We're not ready yet, Bob, for this sojourn into *terra incognita.*" In conducting past-life therapy and observing some of the astonishing cures that often result, I still often wonder about my true role in the therapeutic process. If at least some current-life problems really are a penance for previous-life transgressions, who am I to defy or attempt to overrule that destiny, that karma? But I also reflect that perhaps I serve as a keeper of the keys at the patient's prison gate, opening that gate when the transgressor has paid his or her debt. I would like to be able to let everyone out when they wanted to, but that decision is up to a higher authority.

Frankie eventually dropped out of therapy when the terms of his insurance settlement dictated that he would have to pay for sessions out of his own pocket. But then, his rages were less frequent, although I could not say he was cured. I later explored past-life therapy in much more benign settings and have utilized it with enormously encouraging success. Yet, my inner voice tells me, "Do not call Frankie back. You are a healer, not a magician, and you possess no magic to transform him. He has to do what he has to do." I have learned from painful experience to heed that voice.

I can only work with the tools that have been given to me. I now believe that not everyone—or perhaps more accurately, not every soul—will be cured in this lifetime. I, too, will do what I have to do. I will continue to open the gate but only for those for whom it is supposed to be opened.

25 ✧ Reflections on Mass-Hypnosis Regression

R egressions and even past-life regressions and healings can occur in large gatherings as well as in private, one-on-one psychotherapeutic settings. The procedure must be cautious and somewhat delicate, since the therapist performing mass hypnosis hardly wants to unleash an auditorium full of tortured souls reliving ancient pains. Cautious though I must be, when I present a lecture on past-life therapy, I usually include a brief, gently guided reincarnation exercise, and I often conclude with a "healing."

I will share with you a letter I received from a member of the audience at one such lecture. It serves to exemplify the types of experiences a person can have even in a group setting, surrounded by literally hundreds of other people. In fact, many believe that the group atmosphere is an enhancement to healing. This would be comparable to what often transpires in religious ceremonial gatherings, particularly in those at which the acceptance of faith healing is strengthened by the number of people all experiencing and sharing beliefs and reactions.

The woman who wrote to me mentions *Desiderata* in her letter. Her reference is to a short piece of prose written in 1927 by Max Ehrmann, an Indiana poet. I always end my group meditation with its last paragraph, and I have it printed on the back of my patient appointment cards. I will share that, as well, following Mrs. Ross's letter.

Dear Dr. Jarmon:

I was one of the more than 450 people in your audience at Virginia Beach last November. Knowing something of the multiple demands . . . which impact upon people, I have resisted writing you until this morning. Some spirit suggests that I should go ahead and give you the opportunity of knowing the experiences you enabled this one person to add on her eighty-three-year-old journey.

I have had experiences with guided imagery, meditation, and a range of workshops and therapy. When you started to lead us in the past-life regression imagery using a bridge, my visualization was different from earlier experiences. I was struck by how far away the bridge was, how very long and narrow it was, the sense that I would not have time to reach it and cross it in the time your voice offered. Still, I managed to arrive at the end of it and found I was coming off a rude wooden, makeshift structure. I looked down at my feet and found that I was a very stocky man with rough hide, stiff and uncured, cut and folded around my feet and legs, open in the front and tied . . . on my feet and legs . . .

I was holding a huge club, roaring with anger, facing trees surrounding the area, threatening someone, knowing that I would pound him murderously; at the same time, wary of the danger that lurked immediately behind the trees. Your voice called us back. There is that in me that is very glad to have the sense of primitive rage fully experienced in that body. I have worked through a great deal of anger in different ways in my life, and know myself to be at a very different place today. In some way it was like a gift to be aware of the enormous power existing in that emotional state, and to know that it has been to a considerable extent transmuted in my life experiences. In writing this now, I see that it has helped me voice why I felt the experience as such a gift.

The second event I experienced—in some ways of greater importance to me—was in your healing meditation bringing us out of the regression. The telling takes longer than the experience.

You had led us in a relaxation and then suggested that we see a beam of white light over our heads. I was experiencing a very strong white light beaming straight down over my head when suddenly a beam of energy/light elbowed its way in at an angle from the side . . . familiarly like my husband's energy. I was saying in my head, "Oh, Phil, let me have my own image," when your voice began to read and came to, "You are a child of the universe—." Phil died in 1978. One of his favorite sayings was "You are a child of the universe." He cherished the *Desiderata* and had several copies around.

These words on paper cannot begin to communicate the power and synchronicity of the moment, and it was still so funny that I have laughed about it

as well. Phil was an extroverted person with an energy field that could make people feel pushed around. I have told a few people who knew him about the experience. We laugh and feel awe at the same time, for it was so characteristic of him. This is to thank you for that gift, too.
Sincerely yours,

Mary Lou Skinner Ross

The following brief passages from *Desiderata,* including its final paragraph, are indeed relevant to the way we perceive ourselves and our experiences, particularly within the context of psychotherapy but also with regard to all of life's experiences:

Go placidly amid the noise and haste, and remember what peace there may be in silence. As far as possible without surrender be on good terms with all persons. Speak your truth quietly and clearly; and listen to others, even the dull and ignorant; they too have their story . . .
Many fears are born of fatigue and loneliness. Beyond a wholesome discipline, be gentle with yourself. You are a child of the universe, no less than the trees and the stars; you have a right to be here. And whether or not it is clear to you, no doubt the universe is unfolding as it should. Therefore be at peace with God, whatever you conceive Him to be, and whatever your labors and aspirations in the noisy confusion of life keep peace with your soul. With all its sham, drudgery and broken dreams, it is still a beautiful world. Be careful. Strive to be happy.

Mary Lou now has a deepened sense of knowing—one

that she did not have before, though Phil, her husband who was so much in love with life, exerts a presence and guidance that has never left her. She need not fear that she will ever be alone.

26 ✧ Spirit Attachment and Spirit Releasement Therapy

A book that discusses the soul, or spirit, in the context of psychotherapy needs to include at least some comment about the concept of spirit attachment and what is known as spirit releasement therapy. This should probably begin with a clarification of nomenclature, which scrupulously avoids the terms *possession* and *exorcism*, although some therapists refer to "clinical depossession" as a synonym for releasement.

Dr. William Baldwin, a prominent advocate of this therapeutic modality, has explained the choice of terminology in an audiocassette and in his book, *Regression Therapy, Spirit Releasement Therapy*. "The entire concept of spirit interference or attachment," he explains, "met with superstitious resistance to the ominous specter of demonic possession and exorcism as depicted in the movie *The Exorcist* . . . The title or designation for the work needed to be descriptive, inclusive, and accurate, yet distinctly different from and not suggestive of demonic spirit possession or the stylized religious rituals of classic exorcism."[1]

Thus, the phenomenon is designated "attachment" rather than "possession." The word *release*, as Dr. Baldwin notes, carries the essence of the therapy, and adding the suffix *ment* indicates the *process* of releasing.

Now for the harder questions: What (as precisely stated as possible) do the terms denote, and is there any validity to the concept?

The theory begins with the tenet that each of us has a soul, or spirit, and when the body dies the spirit must go somewhere. If this transition occurs without impediments, the soul departs into the tunnel of light and toward the "oneness," but there are other possibilities. The spirit may remain earthbound.

It is believed that in some instances the soul fails—at least initially—to perceive that its body has died; or it may refuse to proceed into the tunnel of light because it has (or feels it has) an unfinished task on earth or feels unworthy or even afraid of returning to the "oneness." Or it may feel a special connection—an affinity— with a living person, stemming from any emotion from love to hate. There are even some theorists who hold that the soul of a drug addict or alcoholic may continue to yearn for drugs or liquor and may seek to invade a living person in order to feed the addiction. There are also those who believe that an earthbound soul sometimes feels an overwhelming affinity for a place and its past associations, rather than for a living person; hence, an explanation of ghosts and haunted houses, a famous example being the ghost of Abraham Lincoln, said to dwell in the White House.

Can any of these things be possible? Logic indicates

that there may never be a definitive answer concerning the reality of such phenomena, but logic also indicates the possibility, however bizarre it may seem. Records and reports suggest that more than eight million Americans have had a near-death experience in which the soul left the body and returned. If the soul can do that, why can it not also, under certain circumstances, turn back from the tunnel and enter another person's being? According to Dr. Baldwin, who has made a study of the subject, "in ninety percent of societies worldwide, there are records of possession-like phenomena."[2] He also cites "extensive clinical evidence which indicates that discarnate beings, the spirits of deceased humans, can influence living people by forming some sort of connection and causing physical and emotional problems."[3]

The theory postulates that such a disembodied consciousness, or spirit, having merged somehow with the subconscious mind of its living host, is like an invisible parasite, exerting some degree of control over the host's mind and, in some instances, the body as well. A great many people may be parasitized in this way, but most are unaware of the invasion, of the presence of one or more spirits in addition to their own. They are aware only of physical or mental symptoms of unknown cause, such as sudden, inexplicable impulses or behavior. For that matter, an attached spirit may in some cases be present without producing noticeable symptoms. The unawareness (even when symptoms are manifest) is, according to Baldwin, a major factor in the reluctance to accept the concept of "discarnate interference."

So, too, is the belief that any such symptoms stem from more familiar machinations of the psyche. One clinician may suspect that chronic fatigue is caused by the stress and energy drain of spirit attachment, while others diagnose it as the result of known physical or emotional disorders. Total attachment and dominance by the infiltrating spirit, a "take-over" of the host, might cause a drastic personality change, a suppression of the original personality, but so can known dysfunctions and illnesses.

Thus, many therapists would ascribe the symptoms of spirit attachment to a schizoid syndrome or to a multiple-personality disorder, which causes a person at times to speak and behave in a manner entirely different from his or her normal pattern.

On the other hand, this type of familiar, easier to accept diagnosis can be frustrated by an afflicted person who hears voices (internal or external) or sees images of unknown faces or figures, or reveals other such symptoms, *but exhibits no other psychotic symptoms or behavior.* If this is "simply" hallucination, what causes it, and are we so knowledgeable that we can state categorically that spirit attachment is not the explanation?

My personal experience with this therapy is very limited. I feel, however, that it may be worthwhile to tell you about the one patient I helped to take into this *terra incognita* when other therapeutic stratagems had failed to complete his cure.

My patient was Chris, a hard-working family man in his late thirties who had decided to find out whether psychotherapy could relieve his nebulous feelings of anxiety and self-doubts as well as mounting marital discord. During several months of therapy, we uncovered quite a few repressed memories. He remembered that during his childhood he had been sexually abused, and he remembered two near-death experiences that his conscious mind had blocked out. In the course of working through those near-death experiences, he was able to comprehend and thus shed anxieties that amounted to mild phobias. He seemed to be making good progress when we hit an odd and unexpected barrier, an unnamed something present in his mind that prevented further headway. One day as I began to counsel him, he said, "Wait, I have to tell you about this thing I feel. There's something in the middle of my head that needs to come out."

Before the time came for his next appointment, he called me. He had become increasingly troubled about the thing he perceived inside his head, and now he added that it was exerting some kind of control over him. He had an uneasy sense that it was something evil.

For years, he had listened in his church to priests warning parishioners about the dangers of the forces of evil, and now Chris was beginning to feel that this evil was in no way allegorical but an actual, palpable force that had somehow invaded his being. Given the litany of traumas he had endured in childhood, he wondered if during one of those times of weakness and suffering something evil had seized the opportunity—that is, his vulnerable state—to infiltrate his body and mind.

I had never so much as considered the possibility that an emotional disturbance could be caused by a resident spirit, evil or otherwise. A cancer patient weakened by chemotherapy is at risk of becoming a host for pathological bacteria, but bacteria are, after all, *physical* entities. Physicians are not inclined to regard intangible entities in the same way, and it had never occurred to me that a weak state of body, mind, or spirit could be similarly vulnerable to attack and infiltration by uninvited spirits.

Since Chris viewed the "forces of evil" in the light of his church's teachings, I suggested that he talk to his priest about his concern. He told the priest he was afraid that the devil or some minion of evil—a servant of the devil, so to speak—had taken hold of him, that perhaps during one of those times when he had been near death or wishing he were dead, a hostile spirit had attached itself to his soul. He told the priest he had never taken the warnings from the pulpit literally, but now he did and wanted to know how to combat the evil presence. (In the Bible there are accounts of men possessed by "unclean spirits," and Christ directs those spirits to leave their hosts. In Mark, Chapter One, he releases such a spirit from a man in Capernaum. In Mark, Chapter Five, Christ releases multiple spirits that are afflicting a man from Gerasene and thereby heals him. In 1993, Pope John Paul II was reported to have worked an exorcism on a man attending one of his masses.)

"What did the priest advise?" I asked him.

"He looked at me as if I were crazy. He actually backed away. He told me I should see a good psychiatrist. These guys can talk a good story, but they don't really believe their own preaching."

"You sound angry," I said, "or bitter. That's natural, but why condemn the priesthood or the church? Maybe your particular priest doesn't believe or doesn't take it literally—or does he believe it? Maybe it scares him. That would be natural, too."

We pursued the problem no further that day, but Chris had a session with me a few days later, and I started to put him into a trance. What happened next was unsettling. No sooner had he closed his eyes than his voice and demeanor changed markedly. An angry voice issued from him. It was his voice, yet it was not. "He's mine!" the voice declared, loud and defiant. As these words came from him, Chris's fists clinched and his arms and legs trembled. His neck stiffened and his lips tightened in what I must describe as a snarl, baring his teeth.

Keeping my composure as well as I could, I said in a gentle but firm tone, "Let God's light shine on you and in you. We're all children of God."

The voice came again, more adamant and foreboding than before. "He's mine. I'm not leaving. I—will—not—leave!"

Valerie Melusky, a psychologist friend of mine, had told me of her experiences with such cases. She had written her doctoral thesis on spirit depossession—releasement—and had given me some suggestions about handling such situations. Remembering her advice, I told the voice: "Let go of this place where you need no longer be and go into the light. You will be guided there. We all come from God, and no matter how bad we have been, we all get to go back to God, the source of all."

The voice remained defiant and adamant: "I will not leave."

I decided not to press harder, at least for the present. I told the voice it could rest now, but soon, at the appropriate time, it would be free to go back into the love of God.

I was far from certain what I was dealing with. Perhaps in probing through the surface of a patient who appeared to be simply neurotic, I had unleashed a psychotic. Perhaps I was witnessing all the pent-up anger caused by the patient's childhood abuse and pain.

I eased Chris slowly out of trance and spent some time giving him healing affirmations of God's love. When he seemed ready to discuss what had just taken place, I asked him what he thought the voice represented. Whatever it was, he said, he wanted it out—and quickly, as quickly as possible. So did I, but I wanted to be sure we had any and all appropriate preparations made. A basic rule for good medical care is never to perform an elective procedure without being prepared to deal with its possible complications. If, indeed, spirit releasement therapy was called for, I knew where to find help. With Chris's permission, I phoned Valerie and told her what had transpired. She said it did sound like spirit attachment and offered her assistance.

In preparation, she had two lengthy telephone conversations with the patient and then called me back. We agreed to perform the spirit releasement procedure together and to enlist the help of a nurse who had a deep interest in this field, had had her own psychic experiences, and was someone with whom I had previously worked. There was concern that the patient might experience an intense emotional eruption.

The nurse would monitor the patient's pulse and blood pressure and, if necessary, assist in applying restraints that (again with Chris's permission) I would have on hand. In addition, Chris asked two priests to attend the session, to help or at least be present, but they declined, perhaps feeling that the procedure would be a lay exorcism. I must confess that I did not feel confident of success. I had witnessed an alleged spirit releasement only once before, and it had not been especially impressive. I am not sure that much took place except that the patient had received a lot of attention from the five therapists gathered there. Naturally, I was concerned that this might prove to be the case with Chris and equally concerned that it would not!

The psychologist, the nurse, and I met with Chris in his home. We decided he would be most comfortable in a familiar setting. Afterward, if necessary, he could rest in his own bed. Perhaps he would need a sedative or would at least want to nap.

For two hours, the psychologist merely spoke in a soft voice to him about his problems and about the procedure we were about to undertake. Then she hypnotized him and entreated any attached spirit to identify itself. I am purposely avoiding here any detail of the process. I would not want readers to take this description as a primer for spirit releasement and try to do it themselves.

For some time, she could not elicit a response from the voice I had heard, and about a half an hour passed without obvious progress. Then, at last, Chris spoke in a strange voice. "I am Gregory," the voice announced, "and I am happy here. I will remain."

Quietly but firmly, we debated with "Gregory" about why it was time for him to depart from Chris and go back to the light. The voice argued stubbornly that he had no wish to depart, as we continued to firmly urge otherwise. At one point, Chris began to thrash and cough as the nurse continued to monitor his pulse and blood pressure. The voice grew angrier as we persisted.

I readied the restraints I had brought, but then I thought of something else I had— something that might, in this case, be more effective.

From my bag, I took an item that is not regularly issued to medical doctors. It was a small bottle that I had filled with holy water at my church that morning. A lifetime of religious teaching and experience had conditioned Chris to accept the power inherent in rituals such as the sprinkling of holy water, and I felt it might have a favorable effect, a tranquilizing effect, if not something more. Of course, I had no way of knowing how "Gregory" would react to it, but with the restraints at hand, that was a small risk worth taking.

I sprinkled some of the holy water on his forehead and with my finger made the sign of the cross while I talked about peacefulness of spirit and love from God. I wondered to myself what my Jewish grandmother would have thought of my actions. I decided she probably would have said, "Votever voiks."

The thrashing continued briefly and then, quite abruptly, subsided. There was a moment of silence, and then, in his normal voice, Chris made a quite unexpected and very welcomed announcement: "It's gone."

"Gregory" had left him. A calm seemed to have wafted into the room, perhaps a general feeling of relief. The psychologist asked if there were any other spirits still inhabiting Chris. He mumbled that there were six more.

We had been at it now for three hours. She had warned me that the procedure could be long, tedious, and messy. All the same, we decided to keep going for a while in the hope of giving Chris total and lasting relief. During the next hour, we addressed the other entities, asking them to identify themselves and urging them to leave as Gregory had departed, into the light. One by one, they did so.

I was still unsure what I had witnessed and participated in. Was it all just a processing of vivid imagination or had seven discarnate spirits of the dead actually freed themselves from Chris's body and gone up into that tunnel of light? Of course, we did not and could not know the answer, nor was an answer required. This was not, after all, a scientific experiment but a therapeutic attempt, and if our patient was better, we could be happy with the result.

Chris *was* better. After a year of follow-up therapy, he continued to report that the "block" of possession he had felt never returned. After that single session, he had a general peacefulness about him that he never had before.

I encouraged him to find the time each day to "put himself in the light," by way of thanking God and asking for continued peacefulness. After a few weeks he apparently dropped that practice. Three years later I saw him with some new frustrations and anguish with which he is still dealing, but his wife told me that the intense anger had never returned after that "releasement" session.

Some therapists believe that multiple spirit attachment is the explanation for multiple personalities. Others claim it is the other way around—that multiple personality gives an illusion of multiple spirit attachment. Many therapists would argue that neither condition exists.

I would be the first to admit that I do not fully understand all the ramifications of spirit releasement therapy. It would seem to warrant further investigation; however, it needs to be explored carefully. I would not encourage anyone to delve into this process with anything less than the greatest deal of caution. I know that the little angel on my shoulder seems to be saying, "Let this one go for now, Bob. There are other fish to fry."

27 ✧ Karmic Interludes and the Road Ahead

In this book, I have written at length of the soul and past-life therapy and presented a number of case studies that, I hope, have been illuminating with regard to these concepts. I have also written briefly of karma, the principle of causality in Hinduism and Buddhism. As stated in Chapter Twenty-Four, karma has been defined as the resultant ethical consequences of one's acts that fix one's lot in the future existence, the continuous working of every thought, word, or deed throughout eternity in a causal sequence. Karmic commentaries and interpretations have filled books, and the definition just offered is necessarily only a basic and simple one, but it has direct application to the healing of the soul.

It is unfortunate that so many people define it in an even simpler way, as one's unchangeable destiny, as if a person cannot and should not take responsibility for his or her actions and his or her future fate. On the contrary, our thoughts, words, and acts directly influence what is to come in this present life and in future incarnations just as our thoughts, words, and deeds in previous lives influence our present incarnation. Belief in the karmic journey of the soul, with accompanying insight into its ramifications, has been a balm for some of my patients. These journeys do not lend themselves to scientific proof, but the concept most certainly lends itself to the healing of anguish.

One patient who had such insight revealed to me a related concept that cannot be proved but can, nevertheless, bring peace and healing to families mourning the deaths of infants.

This patient was Cathy, forty-two years old, the mother of four, and newly divorced. She had come to me for help in resigning herself to her broken marriage so that she could get on with her life. She was only slightly co-dependent in her relationship with her former husband, Fred, but she was a care-giver by nature and had difficulty turning away from anyone who needed help— as Fred most certainly did.

Clearly discernible beneath Fred's affable surface was a very troubled soul. He suffered from alcoholism and what is sometimes called manic/depressive or bipolar disorder. Cathy had stayed with him as long as she could bear. Al-Anon guidelines would have labeled her efforts to help him as "enabling," that is, enabling him to continue his drinking and excusing or denying his condition rather than letting him deal alone with the consequences of his actions. "Tough love," loving a person enough to be tough with him and tolerate no further misconduct, does not come easily. Family life and finances had deteriorated until there had been no rational alternative to divorce, and very soon after Fred was gone, Cathy came into therapy.

After a session of cognitive—logic-oriented—counseling, Cathy knew clearly what mental steps she had to take to proceed with her life, but her emotional attachment to Fred was not so easily broken. She felt rather as if she had abandoned him. I suggested hypnosis to help her visualize getting on with life without him.

She had had experience with meditation and was able to get into clinical hypnosis quickly. I directed her to go back in her mind—her memory—to the reason why she felt so forcefully compelled to take care of Fred. Her facial expression became intense, and for about half a minute, she wept. When her sobbing stopped, her expression changed abruptly, first to a look of surprise and then relief, or peace.

"Oh, my God!" she exclaimed, "It's Fred. My baby is Fred!"

"Your baby?" I said. "What do you see? What do you see happening?" As she explained what she saw, I found the scenario at first surprising but revealing and then bewildering.

In another lifetime, she had been an expectant mother, and when she returned to that previous lifetime she saw herself dying in childbirth. She also saw—perceived—that the infant survived. It was a boy. She immediately realized that it was Fred in a previous incarnation. Quite frequently, people who visualize themselves in past lives also visualize past-life connections with previous incarnations of present-life relatives, loved ones, or friends. That much I understood and was only momentarily surprised. But then she uttered an astonishing and perplexing statement.

"I wanted to stay. How I wanted to stay! To watch over him. But I had to leave. He wasn't even two years old when I had to leave."

I was somewhat confused. How, I wondered, if she had

died in childbirth, had she stayed to watch over her son until he was almost two years old? I asked her what she meant by "staying" and "watching over" the infant. She explained almost casually—matter of factly—that her soul had resisted going to the light, had struggled to remain on the earth plane in order to be with him and guard him. She had felt deeply guilty for dying as he was born and, thus, "deserting" him. But in time, the spirit guides had persuaded or somehow commanded her to depart and go to the resting place.

This, it seemed, would be a useful perspective for her to understand why she had needed to go on caring for her husband, the reincarnation of the son she had borne. I offered healing affirmations that she could not have prevented her own death. It was not her fault she had left her baby, and she had sought him out again in this present life in order to give him help that she had not been able to provide in that previous lifetime. She had now given all the help that could be given, except for one last act—for now it was time to let him go out into the world without further mothering, on his own, to learn the lessons that only his own experiences could provide.

Whether or not all this was absolutely true in a factual sense, she clearly seemed to be accepting it, to be enormously relieved by it. She was healing, and that was what she had come for. But something occurred to me and I decided not to bring her out of trance quite yet. What if I had before me a mind, conscious or subconscious, that possessed some knowledge of death and the afterlife, the soul's experience of survival and subsequent lives and deaths. Perhaps she could answer some questions for me.

Specifically, I was thinking about premature death— not only the death of a young woman in childbirth, which could have easily detectable causes, but the mysterious tragedy of what is known as sudden infant death syndrome (SIDS) or crib death. I cannot say why that occurred to me, since in this case it was the mother who died and not the infant. But I have already stated my belief in some guiding force for each of us—a guardian angel or guiding spirit—and perhaps it was my angel that was what impelled me to ask, "Why is it, Cathy, that sometimes an infant will die unexpectedly, for no apparent medical reason? Do you know?"

"Yes, I know," she said. "Sometimes in a rush to return to the earth plane a soul chooses to come into a body and a life that's not the right one to fulfill its karma. After a little while here, the soul realizes its mistake and leaves its new body."

How wonderful, I thought, what a beautiful explanation of SIDS. Surely this understanding could help bereaved parents cope with their grief and begin to accept their loss.

But the world is not that simple and seldom that kind. On the basis of an interview with a hypnotized person, I could not very well imagine some medical journal publishing a paper by Dr. Jarmon announcing to his fellow physicians: "You have all been looking for the wrong causes—allergic reactions or maldevelopment of the neuronal pathways regulating infant cardiopulmonary response. The truth is so much simpler. The soul finds itself in the wrong body and departs. Stop your research protocols and return your grant money. I have found the mechanism, and it is karma."

No, that is not likely to happen, now or in the future. A truth, an insight, can be a burden as well as a tool of healing. What is to be done with concepts such as this? It is hardly a hypothesis that can be tested by an conventional (hence, widely accepted) means. Essentially, it is what is known as a "null" hypothesis: one that can be demonstrated to be true only by eliminating all other possibilities. This would be like having to prove that dragons do not exist by examining every square inch of the universe and not finding any. Even that would fail to prove the nonexistence of invisible dragons, nor is it possible to prove the existence of an invisible concept such as karma and the reality of spirits or the reality of the guardian angel, the force, that prodded me to ask about sudden infant death syndrome. Yet, we may well be denying ourselves an understanding of our universe by rejecting outright all hypotheses that cannot be tested by orthodox scientific methods.

Most of us retain religious beliefs, in part because we need to believe, to explain to ourselves the inexplicable and to deal with the prospect of physical mortality, in part, I think, because we absorb those beliefs in early childhood and they are beliefs shared by our peers. But I am also convinced that all cultures have religious beliefs of one kind or another simply because God does exist and imbues us with belief. Yet, outside of our widely accepted religious concepts, many of us limit our beliefs to those phenomena which can be detected by the five physical senses: sight, hearing, smell, taste, and touch. A blind person has only four senses, a blind and deaf person only three, and a person who has been blind and deaf since birth has to be informed that colors and sounds exist. Being unable to sense them physically does not mean they have no existence. Why should we assume that five is the optimal number of senses? Perhaps we would need ten or more to be fully aware of all that is going on in the cosmos.

For those who profess to heal, I have come to believe that it is of enormous benefit to accept and integrate the concept of the soul in treating patients, and I shall continue to practice my profession accordingly. Good health should not be viewed as merely the absence of disease but as the more gratifying and fulfilling well-being of body, mind, and spirit. As for life's problems and calamities, they can be viewed as learning opportunities and opportunities for the growth of the soul. That is a much healthier and more productive attitude than cursing the injustice of bad fortune.

The psychotherapist who has some knowledge of the spectrum of psychic experiences and phenomena is in a good position to help a patient separate real from imagined occurrences. I have known patients who suffered needlessly because they were afraid that no one—especially a legitimate therapist—would understand or even believe their out-of-body experiences, near-death experiences, past lives, angelic intervention, or ghostly visitation. Many of these people feared they were losing their sanity. What such people need, I now believe, is a rational approach to the concept of the soul in adjunctive psychotherapy.

This does not mean that we should abandon conventional medicine or psychotherapy. In fact, as I have said elsewhere, established medical treatment must not be bypassed. Meditation is no substitute for a needed appendectomy, and an emotional trauma suffered in a patient's present life rather than in a past life is often the incident that requires the attention.

All the same, the therapist who can work with spiritual concepts while maintaining objectivity and a command of reality can help patients heal in ways that standard psychotherapy does not provide. In this book, I have shared some of my experiences in the use of such healing. As I continue to work, I will continue to learn, and so I must regard some of my findings as tentative. No matter, as long as they help those in need of help.

Certain of my beliefs have grown to be quite positive, however, not in the least tentative, the most important to me being that the major aspect of our existence is immortal. In medicine, we struggle to keep these temporary vehicles for the soul, our bodies, from breaking down and dying. The truth, of course, is that these vehicles must inevitably die.

There is enormous benefit to humankind in preventing or curing physical disease, but the *ultimate* focus should be on building a healthy, productive, and learning existence while we are here on this earth plane. One might well think of it as a school session that is now in progress and will eventually be interrupted but will also eventually be resumed. Death is only a recess, an indeterminate period, one might say, of rest and recuperation for the soul. We expend too much anguish over it, and that anguish can be translated as fear, a waste of vital energy. We will do better to focus on life and accept eventual death as a rest period that will come when it will. Meanwhile, those of us who accept a calling as healers will not be worthy of the term physician if we fail to search for new ways to help our patients when the old modalities have been exhausted and the pathologies persist.

While not risking our patients' well being, we ought to reexamine our own orthodoxy and our smugly comfortable, conventional attitudes and reverence of mechanistic medicine. Albert Einstein said, "The important thing is not to stop questioning. Curiosity has its own reason for existing. One cannot help but be in awe when he contemplates the mysteries of eternity, of life, of the marvelous structure of reality. It is enough if one tries merely to comprehend a little of this mystery every day. Never lose a holy curiosity."

It is also acceptable to acknowledge that there are many things that we do not know. Thomas Jefferson advised that, "Ignorance is preferable to error; and he is less remote from the truth who believes nothing, than he who believes what is wrong."

My favorite commentary, however, on our arrogant ignorance of the workings of psyches or universes is found in John Godfrey Saxe's delightful poem based, I

believe, on an old Sufi parable, "The Blind Men and the
Elephant."

It was six men of Indostan to learning much inclined,
Who went to see the elephant, (though each of
them were blind),
That each by observation might satisfy his mind.

The first approached the elephant, and, happening to fall
Against his broad and sturdy side, at once began
to bawl:
"God bless me but this elephant is nothing but a
wall!"

The Second, feeling of the tusk, cried: "Ho! what
have we here
So very round and smooth and sharp? To me 'tis
mighty clear
This wonder of an elephant is very like a spear!"

The Third approached the animal, and, happening to take
The squirming trunk within his hands, thus
boldly up and spake:
"I see," quoth he, "the elephant is very like a
snake!"

The Fourth reached out his eager hand, and felt
about the knee:
"What most this wonderous beast is like is mighty
plain," quoth he.
"'Tis clear enough the elephant is very like a tree."

The Fifth, who chanced to touch the ear, said,

"E'en the blindest man
Can tell what this resembles most; deny the fact who can,
This marvel of an elephant is very like a fan!"

The Sixth no sooner had begun about the beast to grope,
Than, seizing on the swinging tail that fell within his scope,
"I see," quoth he, "the elephant is very like a rope!"

And so these men of Indostan disputed loud and long,
Each in his own opinion exceeding stiff and strong,
Though each was partly in the right, and all were in the wrong!

So, oft in theologic wars the disputants, I ween,
Rail on in utter ignorance of what each other mean,
And prate about an elephant not one of them has seen!

*   *   *

✧ Epilogue

In 1988, in the coronary care unit of San Francisco General Hospital, a study was undertaken on nearly 400 heart attack patients over a ten-month period. An old and long-abandoned medical adjunct to therapy was reinstituted to see if it could improve patient outcome. The patients were divided into two groups in order to give both an equal balance according to the severities of their conditions.

The results were astounding. The group that received the adjunctive therapy as opposed to the control group had significantly improved outcomes as measured by incidences of complications such as congestive heart failure, cardiopulmonary arrest, pneumonia, need for diuretics, antibiotics, and intubation/ventilation. Whereas 7% of the patients in the control group went into cardiopulmonary arrest, only 2% in the *extra* therapy group did so.

The study was conducted under strictly controlled double-blind guidelines, meaning that neither the patients nor their doctors and nurses knew who was getting the added therapy and who was not.

This apparently remarkable aid to patient recovery has several aspects that currently hinder its widespread use; it is not subject to FDA approval, not expensive, not painful, and not new. Neither does one need a license to administer it nor need to be in the patient's presence during administration!

If this *were* an FDA-approved, eighty-dollar-per-dose, painful, newly developed injection showing these incredible results, physicians would be sued for malpractice for not prescribing it.

Just what was this incredible something? It was prayer.[1]

What was the nature of the therapeutic process at work? Did the minds of those doing the praying connect with their own souls, which in turn connected with the souls of the cardiac patients, which in turn affected physical changes in those patients' bodies? Who can say? But if it worked well and is safe and cost effective, why are we not using this more?

There exists a great reluctance in modern medical science to deal with factors affecting patients' well-being which may elude quantification, predictable access, or simply understanding. We see ourselves as keepers of the gate of modern science, believing that whatever is contained within is almost all that should be allowed in. We scrutinize closely (as we should) any pretenders to that body of knowledge. (I would hate to think that our reluctance might stem from our delicate egos. Could we be so threatened at some deep level over the fact that our patient's $4000-a-day services in a modern coronary care unit mean nothing if that patient's little boy is not praying for him at home?)

Very fortunately, we do not have to make an either/or decision here. We can have the best of both worlds. We can and should keep modern medical modalities in diagnosing and treating diseases of the mind, the body, and the *mind/body*. But we can still and we should concomitantly incorporate that elusive intangible that is very much a part of our universe. It simply stands to reason that if a person's illness is a compilation and amalgam of mind, body, and spirit, then not to address one or two of those factors is to fall short of giving our patients the best possible care.

In writing this book, I hoped that many of you who have known a contact with some aspect of the oneness described here would take heart that there are some of us therapists who are attuned to such phenomena and can work with it. In addition, I hope that other therapists and physicians who might have been actively suppressing that little voice of higher wisdom within will take courage to stand up and be counted and not be afraid to treat their patients with more attention to this aspect of our world. It is unfortunate that most psychotherapeutic training programs have ignored, if not outright discouraged, the philosophical and spiritual component to therapy.

As for myself, I can now better appreciate the twists and turns that my career path has taken. The more I see, the more I learn, and the more I realize how little we really know. Gone now are the days when I believed I could nearly master an understanding of the psyche. Gone, too, is the sense of failure when a patient's recovery is less complete than hoped for, and gone is the prideful sense of triumph when a patient heals. I know now that I do not work alone. I do the best I can with what I am given, and if the patient is not yet ready to be relieved of suffering, then the suffering will continue. But if it is the patient's time to heal, then it is my obligation and privilege to facilitate that healing.

This is not a new attitude in medicine by any means, but I had to live it to appreciate it. Being a caring human being, I still feel badly when a person who has come to me for help attains less than a full recovery.

But there has come to me a greater personal revelation about my work. One day, when I was fourteen years old, I knew I was going to be a physician. It was as if it were not even a matter of choice. I did not, however, relish the prospect of an exhausting lifestyle with long hours of often frustrating work. I saw our family doctor attend to the people of our town, putting in eighteen-hour days. I am not a lazy person, but I could sense that a physician's life had the potential for more agony than ecstasy.

Throughout my medical training, I was always more fascinated by how the patient as a human being was dealing with his or her disease than by the pathophysiology of the malady itself. The "congestive heart failure in bed 105 B" was to me, first and foremost, a husband and father of three who was despondent over the thought of having perhaps seen his last Christmas. We had gone into medicine to relieve suffering, and too often instead we found that we were prolonging agony.

In Chapter Five, I told the story of Anna and her past-life experiences. Though I did not know it at the time, when Anna came into my office, she opened the door to my understanding of the real purpose of my work. In Chapter Six, I referred briefly to a previous incarnation of my own, which would not have been discovered without Anna's revelations. Now, let me tell you a bit more about my own past-life experiences and how fate—or my karma—has engineered a focus to my career.

Even before Anna reexperienced her previous lives,

there were indications that events prior to her twenti-eth-century existence were exerting an influence on her. While she was experiencing the cessation of menses and developing the abdominal pain characteristic of ectopic pregnancy, she was also having unexplained emotional reactions. As she came out of deep trance, she would of-ten say, "I'm sorry." When I asked her what she felt sorry about, she did not know. Then, one day after a particu-larly deep trance, she looked long and pitifully into my eyes and said in a profoundly remorseful tone, "I'm so sorry for what I did to you!"

When I asked her what she meant, she had no idea. I put her back into trance and asked her to *see* why she felt so sorry. Here is what she described.

"I see the hands of an old woman. They're raw and shriveled. She's holding a baby . . . I love that baby so, I can't stand to hear it cry like this." Anna began to weep as she spoke. "I smell olive oil," she said.

Her reference to olive oil was intriguing. After recent hypnotic sessions, she had told me she detected this odor but did not know where it came from. Scent is something we cannot consciously imagine clearly. For example, you can close your eyes and easily imagine—remember and see—what a banana looks like, but you will have difficulty clearly imagining its smell. Acute odor awareness is a good indicator that the hypnotic subject is operating at a subconscious level. Now, for the first time, Anna was connecting this odor to a particular scene or event.

"The baby is crying because I have no milk to give it. I'm too old, and it's so tiny."

I felt a deep pity for the pangs of this old woman, and then realized I was becoming emotionally involved in what seemed to be an imaginary scenario. But my patient's sorrow was real.

I asked her to describe the setting. It sounded like the

Middle East during biblical times. I asked her to see the time and place more precisely, but she was aware only that she was in a village. I asked what her name was, and as I did so, I thought to myself that she would probably come up with the name Sarah to fit the Biblical scene. "Sarah," she said, and I thought, "I knew it. She'll say the baby's name is David. I don't want to ask her because when she says, 'David,' I'll know I shouldn't have known that. I suddenly had the intense knowing that if I stepped onto this path, there would be no going back."

It also occurred to me that perhaps I was getting carried away, experiencing the transference and countertransference of therapist involvement with a patient. But I realized this was only my ploy to avoid or deny what was happening. I knew I had to ask her the child's name, and I knew what her answer would be.

I asked, and she said, "David." My heart sank. She went on to relate the following story.

Because of her age, she—that is, Sarah—was unable to nurse her baby. With her tiny infant crying for nourishment in her arms and the woman heartsick because she could not feed it, she let other women in the village talk her into giving up the child. The baby, they convinced her, would surely die unless Sarah turned it over to them. They could find women to wet-nurse the child if she would allow them to keep it as their own. Sarah hated the prospect of giving up her newborn child, and she did not trust these women to care for her son, but she felt she had no choice.

I asked her what became of the child, and she said he was taken to another village where he grew up and eventually worked as a healer. My reaction to her account vacillated between relief, wonder, disbelief, and a sense of foolishness for being gullible. But what was uppermost in my thoughts was the growing conviction that I was getting into something unexpected and strange, with the potential for discoveries that I felt needed exploration.

When Anna came out of trance and as I started to retell her story, she glanced down and felt her blouse. There was a discharge coming from her nipples. She was as dumbfounded as I was. She phoned me later that day to tell me that by the time she had reached home her blouse was soaked.

"What *is* going on?" she said.

I had no good explanation. She was a nurse, and I reminded her of the condition known as pseudocyeses— false pregnancy. It sometimes happens that a woman who wants very much to be pregnant or, conversely, greatly fears becoming pregnant develops many of the signs of pregnancy. There may be abdominal enlargement, weight gain, cessation of menses, and morning sickness. These symptoms may disappear with hypnotic therapy.

There never was any good explanation for this in my medical training, except that it was another example of how the mind and body operate together. Women, it seemed, were more susceptible than men to manifestations of the close mind/body connection. The ancients believed that a woman's emotions resided in the uterus and the word *hysteria* is derived from the Greek *ysters*, meaning uterus. (The removal of the uterus is called a hysterectomy.) It is interesting that in recent years modern medicine has begun to acknowledge that a woman's emotional state seems to undergo a change after a hysterectomy.

Anna herself was somewhat bewildered but not particularly fearful of whatever was going on. For my part, however, I was wishing that I felt on firmer ground.

As I worked with her over the course of the next few months, more of her past lives surfaced. Her therapy was not very intense, and much of the time I wondered if our sessions were not even more beneficial for me—for my enlightenment—than they were for her. On more than one occasion I mentioned this to Anna. I did not want to take advantage of the situation in any way. However, she always replied that she was very comfortable with what we were doing, was benefitting from it, and if I could derive some benefit too, so much the better.

I had been working with her for almost a year before we heard about Dr. Brian Weiss's research and writings on past-life therapy. After we met, he encouraged me to have my own past-life regression done, as he thought it might help me in my work. Anna had visualized me in a number of her previous lifetimes, and I was intrigued by the prospect of viewing these existences for myself.

Shortly after Anna, Brian, and I got together in New York, I received a note from her cancelling her next appointment. She said that, having gotten Brian and I together, she felt her purpose for coming into my life was now fulfilled. It was as if unable to nurture and sustain me in a prior life, she had returned to provide for me what she had failed to do before.

I never saw her again.

However, my efforts at achieving past-life visions of myself were frustrating. I had attempted these regressions on three occasions during mass inductions at past-life seminars, including one conducted by Dr. Weiss at a conference of the Association for Research and Enlightenment. I had yet to experience anything. Then, at that same A.R.E. seminar, one of the presenters asked if I would do him the favor of regressing him. I did, and afterward he asked if I would like him to reciprocate. As it turned out, he was so exhausted after our session that he had difficulty hypnotizing me, and instead he asked a colleague to do it.

I went into trance rather quickly, and apparently began to see some scenes from the past. I say apparently because, like most subjects' first encounters with these experiences, I had doubts flying in and out of my consciousness. Most people ask themselves, "Am I just making this up—imagining it?" Often, there is no way to tell.

Be that as it may, I saw myself in three distinct lifetimes. One was my life as a healer in the ancient temple where Brian and Anna worked with me—an experience described in Chapter Six. I saw myself fall over in the garden pool and die of an apparent heart attack some time after the two others had died. I was weary of the work of healing. I had been working alone and, no matter how many of the sick I tended to, there were always more who needed help. I was not sorry to die. It was a relief to know my work was finally over, and I felt joy at seeing those two dear friends waiting for me in the light.

In the scene that came to me from the second life, I was a Union Army surgeon during a Civil War battle. It was a typical combat scene, with wounded men lying on the ground moaning, screaming, dying. Again I was frustrated and exhausted by my work. I looked across the battlefield and saw, on a farmland hilltop, my medical counterpart in the Confederate forces tending to the soldiers our Union troops had shot. I thought it such a terrible waste. All these young men ought to be back at their own homes, tending their farms and courting their young ladies instead of destroying one another's lives in this farmer's fields.

I wondered, what if both armies let the medical officers write the orders of the day and plan the campaign strategies? We might simply say "About face! All you boys just go on home now. It's time again to take part in life; there's no joy in taking part in death. Grow up healthy, take care of yourselves, and have wonderful lives." I thought my Confederate counterpart would probably concur.

Then, as I looked around at our hilltop strewn with dying men, I saw a young soldier lying on the ground, propping himself up on his left elbow. Unlike so many of the other wounded who were moaning or crying out for help, this man had a peaceful smile on his face. It occurred to me when I saw him that this seemed to be a friend of mine, Howard Schnabolk—that is, my friend in my present lifetime as Bob Jarmon. Howard was a wonderful man who loved life and always had a ready smile for everyone. He went to war in Vietnam, flying medical rescue ("dust-off") helicopters, and was killed there while on a rescue mission.

I looked into the eyes of the young Union soldier and could not understand how he could be lying there so content with his horrible wound. As I walked over to him, he waved his hand weakly and smiled again in a way that seemed to say, "It's all right, Doc. Don't bother with me. Go tend to the others, the ones who can use your help. I'll be out of this hell soon, and I'm at peace with that."

I fully understood how he felt. As I slowly turned my exhausted body, mind, and soul to care for the next battle victim, I envied him. He was right. He was getting out of hell, while I had to stay.

The third and last scene I saw was as a young man in a Southern state in the early 1800s. I had been a successful merchant, but now I was on my deathbed. My young wife and three small children were at my bedside. I was dying of throat cancer. I had enjoyed smoking big black cigars without a suspicion of any possible consequences in that era long before medical science had discovered the connection between smoking and disease. The juices from the tobacco had caused cancerous masses to grow in my throat, but neither I nor anyone knew why this monstrous disease was killing me. My wife and children were crying. I was very weak and had great difficulty breathing.

These sensations were so real at the time that I started

to have difficulty breathing and felt my throat swelling. I had sufficient conscious awareness to realize that the therapist hypnotizing me was becoming very uneasy about my condition. I sensed a growing anxiety in her voice, and that held me back from going even deeper into my trance. But still the scene was so real and poignant to me that I cried as I have never cried before or since.

As I felt myself die and sensed my soul being released from my body, I was filled with anger at myself for having given myself this disease—for I was, after all, seeing the scene from the perspective of my present life, fully aware that tobacco had brought on this scourge. I was not feeling sorry for myself, as I felt that I deserved what was happening. My anger and tears were over what I had done to my beautiful, happy family. Leaving my body, looking down at my innocent, crying children and wife, I vowed with all my soul that I would do whatever I could to prevent this thing from happening to any other family.

I must state here that all my life I have disliked the very notion of smoking. It never made sense to me that people would do it. As a child, I used to hide my parents' cigarettes from them. Whenever I saw people smoking, I wanted to accost them and try to talk them out of it. Most of the time, I managed to control that lifelong urge—most of the time. The original reason I took up the study of hypnosis in 1978 was to help people rid themselves of the nicotine addiction. At the time, I thought my motivation was simply that I had seen too much of its carnage in the form of lung cancer, heart attacks, and emphysema while working in emergency medicine. Through the years, I had developed such a reputation as a crusading antismoking doctor that when Ciba-Geigy Pharmaceuticals was planning to market its Habitrol nicotine patch, the company asked me to be one of the physician lecturers who would help to train other physicians to get patients off cigarettes.

Now, my intense, negative feelings about watching people smoke made sense to me in a new and even stronger way. My analytical and skeptical mind, however, questioned whether my imagination had merely concocted this tale of a cigar-smoking father of three to explain to myself why I am so fervent in my attacks on smoking.

To this I must honestly answer: perhaps.

But during my hypnotic regression, my throat certainly felt as if it were closing over, and I was enraged to tears over what I had done to my family. Whether it was imagination or a view of the painful ending of a past life, I saw the long-term effects of nicotine so vividly that I need never feel qualms about pressuring smokers to quit.

Two years later, I was back at the A.R.E. in Virginia Beach, this time as a lecturer at a reincarnation program that I helped initiate. Brian Weiss also participated in the program. As he usually does on such occasions, he led the audience into a group regression. At one point, he instructed us to see where we were in the year 1870.

I immediately saw myself as that weary physician who had survived the Civil War. He told us to seek a sense of how that previous existence might relate to our current lives. Instantly, I was struck by a concept which has profound meaning for me. That nineteenth-century surgeon and that ancient healer had both led laborious, very frustrating, if occasionally gratifying lives. For just as I had discovered in my medical career during this present life, we can often patch people up and work to undo self-inflicted damage, but in the end nobody gets out of this world alive. Physicians to the body—if they are physicians to the body alone—are inevitably frustrated. All of our best work is ultimately futile. At best, medicine fights a delaying action. Death sooner or later finds us all.

At times I am asked how my work in this field has changed my own attitudes.

On a personal level I see this lifetime as one very interesting semester in this university of the universe. I no longer try to understand why an all-loving, all-forgiving God would condemn me to burn in hell eternally for committing some religious "footfault" before I died. I'm just here learning. Every problem or new situation is simply another homework assignment, not meant to punish me, but to provide a learning exercise.

One day the Headmaster will come and release me from school with a message akin to, "You have done enough for now, Bob. Go take a well deserved vacation. Rest, heal, and before you come back, do some reflecting on what it is that you need to work on next time." Of course, if I learn enough this time around, I may not have to come back at all.

Professionally, I still practice medicine, but it is as if I have graduated to a higher level of healing, because now I tend to the patient's spirit, which never dies. The progress we make now does not have to die with the corporal manifestation, the body. The good that I do can be permanent, because now I am also a physician to the soul.

Notes

Chapter 2
The Changing of Minds
1. Owen Gingerich, "How Galileo Changed the Rules of Science," *Sky & Telescope*, March 1993, pp. 32-36.
2. *Holy Blood, Holy Grail*, Michael Baigent, p. 49.

Chapter 4
Clinical Hypnosis
1. William Kroger, *Hypnosis and Behavior Modification*, p. 9.

Chapter 6
A Reunion of Ancient Colleagues
1. Brian Weiss, *Many Lives, Many Masters*, p. 64.

Chapter 22
Terror Under a Full Moon
1. Harold Feldman, M.D., and Robert G. Jarmon, M.D., "Factors Influencing Criminal Behavior in Newark: A Local Study in Forensic Psychiatry," *Journal of Forensic Sciences*, Vol. 24, 1979.

Chapter 26
Spirit Attachment and Spirit Releasement Therapy
1. William Baldwin, *Regression Therapy, Spirit Releasement Therapy*, pp. 157-158.
2. Ibid., p. 9.
3. Ibid., p. 9.

Epilogue
1. Randolph Byrd, "Positive Therapeutic Effects of Intercessory Prayer in a Coronary Care Unit Population," *Southern Medical Journal*, July 1988, Vol. 81, pp. 826-829.

Bibliography

Baigent, Leigh and Lincoln. *Holy Blood, Holy Grail.* New York: Dell Publishing, 1983.

Baldwin, William J. *Regression Therapy, Spirit Releasement Therapy.* Enterprise, Florida: Bethel Publications, 1992.

Fiore, Edith. *The Unquiet Dead.* New York City: Doubleday/ Dolphin, 1987.

Guirdham, Arthur. *Cathars and Reincarnation.* London: The Theosophical Publishing House, 1978.

Hawking, Stephen. *A Brief History of Time.* New York: Bantam Books, 1990.

Head and Cranston. *Reincarnation: The Phoenix Fire Mystery.* New York: Julian Press, 1977.

Hickman, Irene. *Mind Probe Hypnosis.* Kirksville, Missouri: Hickman Systems, 1983.

Kardec, Allan. *The Spirits' Book.* Philadelphia: Allan Kardec Educational Society, 1996.

Kelly, Mary. *The Fireside Treasury of Light.* New York: Simon & Schuster, 1990.

Kroger and Fezler. *Hypnosis and Behavior Modification: Imagery Conditioning.* Philadelphia: J.B. Lippincott Co., 1976.

May, Antoinette. *Psychic Women.* Kirksville, Missouri: Hickman Systems, 1984.

Moody, Raymond. *Life After Life.* New York: Bantam Books, 1976.

Moody, Raymond. *The Light Beyond.* New York: Bantam Books, 1989.

Morse, Melvin. *Closer to the Light.* New York: Villard Books, 1990.

Prabhavananda. *The Bhagavad-Gita.* New York: Penguin Books, 1972.

Strayer, Joseph R. *The Albigensian Crusades.* University of Michigan Press, 1992.

Weiss, Brian L. *Many Lives, Many Masters.* New York: Simon and Schuster, 1989.

Weiss, Brian L. *Through Time into Healing.* New York: Simon and Schuster, 1992.

Whitton, Joel L. *Life Between Life.* New York: Warner Books, 1986.

Zukav, Gary. *The Seat of the Soul.* New York: Simon and Schuster, 1990.

About the Author

Robert G. Jarmon, M.D., a psychiatrist in private practice in Spring Lake, N.J., is on staff at Jersey Shore Medical Center. He graduated from New Jersey Medical College in 1973 with the class honors in psychiatry. Dr. Jarmon's practice focuses on regression hypnoanalysis and the spiritual aspects of healing the mind/body/spirit. He has published numerous articles on these subjects, and has made several appearances on national television. In the 1980's he scripted and narrated the public service radio program "Health Break."

He has served as a member of the board of directors of the American Academy of Medical Hypnoanalysts, editorial review board of the *Medical Hypnoanalysis Journal*, and chairman of the panel on alternative medicine at Jersey Shore Medical Center. He currently serves as president of the 5100 physician member "Alumni of Association of New Jersey Medical School–UMDNJ." Dr Jarmon is co-founder and president of "Healthy Productions," a New Jersey based company that produces self hypnosis recordings to enhance mind/body healing in specific medical conditions.